Infopartnering

Oliver Wight Publications, Inc.

Infopartnering

THE ULTIMATE STRATEGY FOR ACHIEVING EFFICIENT CONSUMER RESPONSE

André Martin

omne͟o

An imprint of
Oliver Wight Publications, Inc.
85 Allen Martin Drive
Essex Junction, VT 05452

Acknowledgments

There are many individuals to whom I owe thanks for help in the writing of this book. I wish to thank in particular Jim Andress. Without Jim's trust, help, and constant support, this book would not have been possible. He was the man who believed in me in 1974 while I learned, developed, tested, and implemented the first DRP/MRP II system in industry. In June 1990, Jim and I shared a vision of totally integrating a distribution pipeline from the end of the production line to the retail store shelf and we teamed up to make it a reality. Jim's business acumen, patience, and great leadership skills are not easily matched in the business world.

Darryl Landvater, consultant and educator, with whom I have worked as a business associate for almost 20 years never gave up on me and now is helping me achieve our vision. Darryl convinced me to write this book and helped fine tune the implementation chapter as well as polish up several sections of the book. Michel Leroux (my business conscience) kept my spirits up during the tough times and helped immensely with ensuring the consistency of terms and the development of the glossary. Ted File who was kind

Acknowledgments

enough to provide a sanity check on the retail side, and Steve Bennett, a professional writer who took the writings of a French Canuck and translated them into readable form. I also wish to thank Gian Fulgoni, Walt Goddard, Rich Sherman, and Jerry Golup. I asked these gentlemen to critique the manuscript and they provided priceless feedback that helped to improve the book. Then there were those very special people at Giant Foods: Dick Schoening, Dave Herriman, Tony Street, Loren Johnson, and Bill Woodside. Finally, there was Joe Andraski at Nabisco and Joel Lemmer at Kellogg who believed in me and stuck it out. I owe a great deal to these fine individuals.

At last, but certainly not least, there is my dear wife Regine who, for the fourth time, put up with me while I wrote or updated a book—on airplanes, in hotel rooms, on weekends, and on vacation. She made great sacrifices and had plenty of reasons to walk away from it all but stuck it out instead. I am forever indebted to her.

Contents

List of Figures and Tables

Preface

This book is the result of a 16-year campaign. In 1975, as director of manufacturing and distribution operations for Abbott Labs in Canada, I developed and implemented the first totally integrated and seamless distribution/manufacturing resource planning and scheduling system in industry.

In 1978, I decided to expand the use of our system outside our company by first integrating it with our single largest account, the Vancouver General Hospital (VGH) in Vancouver, British Columbia, Canada. The idea was to install our DRP system at the VGH and help its people manage and control inventories and replenishment from our DC. The distribution pipeline would have consisted of connecting the VGH electronically (a dedicated line at the time) to our Vancouver DC, which was already connected to our central DC in Montreal, which in turn was connected to our factory. I had to abandon this idea due to the prohibitive costs associated with electronic data transmissions using a 3,000 mile dedicated line. But I never abandoned the dream of one day integrating a distribution pipeline.

In 1983, I published my first book on Distribution Resource Planning (DRP) and launched a campaign to get people thinking in terms of the universal application of DRP. Today, that effort continues and is supported by the results of my consulting at more than 100 companies that cover the spectrum from manufacturers to wholesaler/distributors to retailers, and range in size from small, single-plant operations to giant, multinational corporations. They include consumer product companies such as Procter & Gamble and Colgate-Palmolive, chemical processors such as ICI, computer manufacturer Digital, pharmaceutical manufacturers such as Bristol-Myers and Stuart Pharmaceuticals, wholesaler/distributors such as ServiStar, Mass Merchandisers, Inc., and Bowman Distribution, and giant retailers such as Sears, Giant Foods, and Price Chopper. But whether they make or sell microchips or potato chips, those companies that have managed their purchasing, manufacturing, and logistics in an integrated fashion have enjoyed significant reductions in their operating costs and inventory investments and have experienced dramatic improvements in their customer service.

In June 1990, I teamed up with James G. Andress to create LogiCNet. For almost two years, I toured the United States and Canada and visited with such companies as Wal-Mart, Kmart, Procter & Gamble, Nabisco Foods, Kellogg, Quaker Oats, Kroger, Nestlé Carnation, Campbell Soup, Hunt-Wesson, Dominck's, Von's, H.E. Butt, Giant Foods, Frito-Lay, Super Value, Kraft General Foods, Lever Brothers, Dial, Ocean Spray, and many others. As luck would have it, in 1992 we signed on three of the finest companies I have ever worked with to pilot our vision of a totally integrated distribution pipeline: Giant Foods, Nabisco Foods Group, and Kellogg. As I write these lines, the vision is being fulfilled and is becoming a reality. Today, there is a new name for it, it's called Efficient Consumer Response (ECR).

What Is Infopartnering?

Infopartnering is a process that integrates an entire distribution pipeline using proven concepts and principles applied successfully in retail, wholesale, and manufacturing companies. Infopartnering focuses on the demand side of the supply chain and can therefore be thought of as the demand chain that drives the supply chain.

Infopartnering applied properly will help you achieve the Efficient Consumer Response (ECR) vision across any given trade channel. The objectives of ECR have been described as follows:

> The ultimate goal of ECR is a responsive, consumer-driven system in which distributors and suppliers work together as business allies to maximize consumer satisfaction and minimize cost. Accurate information and high-quality products flow through a paperless system between manufacturing line and checkout counter with minimum degradation or interruption both within and between trading partners.*

---

* Efficient Consumer Response by Kurt Salmon Associates Inc., January 1993 Copyright © 1993 by UCC/GMA/FMI/NFBA/AMI.

Vision—The ECR System

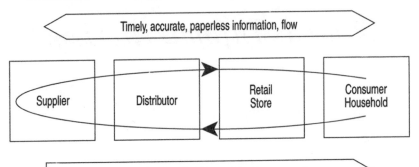

Introduction:
From Marketing Pipe
Dreams to High-Velocity
Distribution Pipelines

"It's your wife on line three, Roy."

"Thanks, Al . . . Hi, hon. Sure I can swing by the super-market. Let me just jot down what you're missing for the barbecue. Soft drinks, uh-huh, barbecue sauce, mayo, and tomato paste. And milk, orange juice, and cereal for break-fast, tomorrow. Oh, cat food, too—about twelve cans. No problem, Martha—see you by seven o'clock."

Roy arrives at the bustling supermarket at 6:15 P.M. and makes his way around the various aisles, pleased to find the barbecue sauces and cereals on sale. He commends himself as he passes the candy aisle without so much as turning his head, but by the time he finishes collecting all of the items on his list, his willpower gives way to temptation; after a quick U-turn in the tuna fish aisle he's back in the sweet-tooth section, and with the skill of a world-class basketball player slam-dunks a special eight-pack of his favorite chocolate bar into the cart.

Roy returns to the checkout line, suddenly feeling the effects of a very long day. By the time he reaches the cash register, he feels like he's only running on two cylinders, very glad that he'll soon be sipping a glass of ice tea on his patio and munching a candy bar (or two).

While Roy's energy is flagging, the machinery processing his purchase is humming along at full tilt. And the night is still young for the systems and the teams of people that will take over once the checkout clerk has scanned in the soft drinks and other items Roy needs for his cookout.

As the scanning takes place, the details of the transaction are transmitted electronically from the point-of-sale terminal to the in-store inventory and shelf management systems. This in turn triggers a fascinating series of events: First, the in-store systems automatically adjust the inventory balance for the items that have just been scanned. Then, they carry out a series of planning steps to determine whether product needs to be reordered (in this store, the checkout clerk was trained to scan in each can of cat food, rather than counting the cans and hitting the multiplier key; otherwise, valuable inventory data would have been lost).

By ten o'clock that evening, when Roy is bidding his dinner guests goodnight, the systems have evaluated the inventory of the stores and compared the figure against an ongoing calculated plan for every item in every store, noted any differences between what was expected to happen and what really happened, and adjusted the schedules accordingly. In some cases, items are needed earlier than planned; in other cases, they are needed later.

Some of the products, such as Roy's mayo, barbecue

sauce, tomato paste, and orange juice, have been scheduled for delivery from the supermarket's retail distribution center (RDC). Others, including the soft drinks and milk that Roy purchased, will be supplied by direct store delivery vendors. And still others, such as Roy's chocolate bars, cereals, and cat food have been planned for shipment directly from the manufacturer.

The entire inventory evaluation process and transmission of information has proceeded with the buyers still in control, even though it's happening late at night. The buyers, distribution people, and store operations people have set up rules for replenishing inventories so that well after they have gone home for the day, the latest information can be used to recalculate the schedules for each item in each store throughout the chain.

By 11:00 P.M., the in-store systems have recalculated the entire set of schedules for each item and all stores in the chain (the schedule for the supermarket Roy visited is added to the schedules from other stores owned by the chain, creating a consolidated schedule). While this schedule extends for many weeks into the future, the focus at the moment is on tomorrow. What items need to be picked up from the distribution center (DC) and sent to which stores? This information is extracted from the system, and pick lists are created, identifying the product's location in the DC, and how much to pick for each of the trucks destined for the specific stores; it is even "smart" enough to know which stores can be restocked during the day, and which can only be replenished at night because of traffic and other logistical considerations.

Between 2:00 and 3:00 A.M., the trucks have left the DC and are en route to their various destinations. Once at their respective stores, the vehicles are unloaded in shelf sequence, so staff can simply "walk the aisles" and restock the shelves. By dawn, a number of stores in the chain are already restocked with items from the retail DC and prepared for a fresh round of customers.

So much for the mayo, barbecue sauce, tomato paste, and orange juice. Now consider what happens to the soft drinks and milk, which are handled by the direct store delivery vendors. As the soft drinks and milk were scanned, the system transmitted a message to a geographical "mailbox" shared by various delivery vendors. As in the case of products from the RDC, the system merges data from all of the stores in the chain, and breaks it down by geographic requirements. By 3:00 A.M., people at the direct store delivery operations have begun dialing into the electronic-mail system, and have initiated the process of updating schedules, loading trucks, and delivering to those stores.

The information in the system is incredibly precise. For example, a soft drink bottler has received a schedule that not only identifies specific routes and specific stores but lists the products, the aisle, the shelf slot, and the specific quantities for each shelf. The bottler's drivers have hit the road by 5:00 A.M., and by ten o'clock that morning the shelf is replenished, ready for Roy's next barbecue. Total lapsed time from when Roy walked in the door to the time the shelf was replenished? A little more than 12 hours.

Roy's shopping cart is now accounted for, except the chocolate bars, cat food, and cereal. These items are distributed through an arrangement that, in today's terms, could only be described as unconventional. A number of different manufacturers and retailers, some of which are competitors, participate in a "cross-docking" arrangement. Truckloads of product from several different manufacturers, destined for different stores and in some cases different retail chains, enter the cross-docking facility. Trucks destined for a particular store or group of stores and loaded with products from several different manufacturers leave the facility. Inside, products are unloaded, sorted by store, and reloaded; they are not warehoused or stored, but rather move in and out. Consequently, products move from the manufacturer's plant to the store shelves in record time, with only one handling step in between. The only thing that could be more efficient would be stores ordering truckloads of product direct from the manufacturing plants—and few stores have either the movement or the space to do that.

Information, not inventory, drives this facility. Here's what happens when the checkout clerk scans these items. By 11:00 P.M., the information about today's purchases has been used to update the schedules for the cross-docking facility. Some items are needed sooner than planned; others later. The latest information is used to recalculate the schedules, and then, just as in the case of the retail distribution center, the schedule for tomorrow is extracted and picking lists are produced. The next day, these products are loaded, in the appropriate quantities, onto trucks destined for the cross-docking facility.

Trucks from the factory are scheduled to arrive at the cross-docking facility within a two-hour time window. The window is rigorously adhered to in order to ensure that the products can be quickly unloaded and reloaded onto trucks, each of which has a specific delivery route. When the trucks arrive at the stores on their route, the products are unloaded by shelf and slot. Each day, this process is repeated in a remarkable sequence of lean, efficient, responsive replenishment. In addition, some products have been custom-packaged in the cross-docking facility according to the demographics and rate of sale by store.

Instead of being forced to accept a two- to three-week supply of certain products, the stores on the delivery route can expect exactly a one-week supply—information has supplanted the shipping unit or lot size, so that stores can dynamically receive what they need, based on their needs.

Does all this sound like a dream? On the one hand, it is; the system just described eliminates most of the bottlenecks and practices and thereby has the potential to increase profitability. On the other hand, the technology needed to move product so effectively is readily available, and a number of pioneering retailers and manufacturing companies, such as Giant Foods, Kellogg, and Nabisco, are gaining significant strategic and competitive advantages by creating "information partnerships" that link vendors and retailers in "pipelines" extending from the raw materials to the ultimate point of consumption. And many other companies, in industries ranging from health and beauty care to consumer electronics, are close to implementing info-partnering arrangements through what is popularly known as an "Efficient Consumer Response" (ECR) system that will slash logistics costs and boost customer service levels. Mass merchandisers and price clubs, too, are in hot pursuit of information partnerships, positioning themselves for the enormous benefits that accrue from gathering demographic and geographic data with every purchase and converting it into "actionable information."

Why the interest in information partnerships and ECR? Aside from the obvious benefits derived from a smoothly operating distribution system, the potential savings in costs are staggering. Consider the grocery industry, which is on the cutting edge of the infopartnering revolution. According to a number of studies undertaken by various independent researchers and funded by industry trade associations, grocery supply chain participants can save an estimated $30 to $50 billion annually in reduced inventory costs across the entire distribution pipeline, and drug store health and beauty care segments can save an estimated $7 billion.

In the dry grocery segment, for example, the traditional distribution pipeline typically carries 80 to 110 days' worth of inventory. In the scenario presented above, which is based on a composite of actual businesses, the infopartnering/ECR approach enabled participants in the pipeline to improve market share by having products available in their stores when needed. Retailers were also more competitive because they significantly reduced their costs, both in handling and inventory. In the stores, average inventory dropped to seven days, transit time to three days, and in-plant warehouse to eight days, for a total of eighteen days from factory to retail stores. That represents a four- to fivefold improvement over today's average inventory investment.

Infopartnering and ECR pipelines also offer companies enormous balance sheet and profit and loss benefits: better profitability and market share by reducing lost sales and "rain checks," significant cost reductions by eliminating unnecessary handling steps, and the freeing up of working capital that used to be tied up in distribution channels, warehouses, and the like. As a result, executives in retail, wholesale, and manufacturing organizations can significantly improve their return on capital and profitability.

A less apparent benefit is the effect on retail store shelf

space. Stores are generally forced to live with the package sizes for the products they carry. If a case consists of twenty-four cans of soup, or a pallet of bottled water of forty-five containers, then the stores must either put it all out on the shelves or add cost by storing some in the back and later retrieving it. What if products could be better packaged to match their anticipated "sell" rates? Customer service doesn't suffer because enough stock is maintained for safety, but the excess inventory that took up shelf space or added handling cost is eliminated. This repackaging is one of the activities that can be done at the cross-docking facility, since the destination, and consequently the sell rate, are known as the product passes through the facility.

This book is designed to help your company set up infopartnering arrangements and enjoy significant cost savings and other important benefits. It is based on my twenty-five years of experience helping Nabisco Foods, Kellogg, Heinz, Giant Foods, and numerous others build lucrative information partnerships. In the following pages, I've mapped out the opportunities that await you, as well as the pitfalls that can derail your efforts. Part I, The Infopartnering Advantage, provides a "satellite's-eye view" of the process. Chapter 1 contrasts the traditional ways of doing business with those made possible through infopartnering. Chapter 2 explains how information can be used as a strategic weapon, while Chapter 3 describes the "heart and soul" of infopartnering—distribution resource planning (DRP). Chapter 4 explores how infopartnering and ECR techniques improve promotional planning—and offer tremendous benefits in doing so.

Part II, The Infopartner's Tool Kit, discusses the core

concepts necessary for developing infopartnering arrangements and building ECR pipelines. Each of the chapters describes the key principles and techniques you'll need in order to create an information partnership. Chapter 5 discusses the prerequisites, while Chapter 6 takes a fresh look at data and information; in common parlance, the two are often used interchangeably. As you'll discover, though, in the context of infopartnering, the two are separated by a wide gulf, and the key to building an efficient pipeline lies in bridging the abyss so that data becomes *actionable* information. Chapter 7 discusses the hardware aspect of infopartnering—the role of technology in maintaining the flow of information. The people issues, so critical to success, are covered in detail in Chapter 8. In Chapter 9, you'll find a step-by-step "proven path" methodology for implementing the resource scheduling and planning systems essential to infopartnering and ECR. Chapter 10 discusses the challenges and payoffs awaiting companies that pursue infopartnering/ECR as a total framework for doing business.

An Epilogue picks up the scenario discussed above, but from the perspective of a dozen years into the future. You'll visit the kind of cyberstores that will be feasible within the end of the decade, and probably earlier. You'll learn how twenty-first-century pipeline management will drastically alter the way we think of selling and replenishing product today.

As exciting as infopartnering may be, at the present time it is still in its infancy. Yet I believe that it will become the standard operating practice well before the new millennium actually arrives. Companies that continue to think of themselves as independent entities—unconnected to their partners at either end of the distribution pipeline—will be left in the competitive dust by those that understand their roles in the distribution pipeline. The visionaries will create their own futures, reaping the enormous competitive bene-fits of infopartnering and sailing into the next century on the leading edge of their industries.

André Martin
March 1994
Rosemere, Quebec

PART I

The Infopartnering Advantage

CHAPTER 1

Business as Usual: A Satellite's-Eye View

In business today, everything revolves around meeting or exceeding rising customer expectations, whether the context is a grocery store or a department store. Our imaginary customer Roy, described earlier, enjoyed a high level of satisfaction because the products he wanted were available and offered at the right price. And the supermarket he visited was able to meet, and in some cases exceed, his expectations because it was connected to an electronic central nervous system that controlled the complete distribution pipeline. Within the pipeline, planning activities were electronically synchronized in a seamless system extending across a series of infopartnerships, from retail stores to factories. The scanning that took place at the checkout register drove a process that recalculated *what* products were needed in the stores, *how much* was required, and *when* the product had to arrive. Similarly, the electronic process signaled a series of activities that ultimately determined what products should be available in retailers', wholesalers', and manufacturers' distribution centers, and how much product the factories should make.

Such a partnering approach is a far cry from the typical business arrangement today; few companies work together as infopartners for the good of an entire distribution pipeline. Since old habits and assumptions are the biggest stumbling blocks to creating infopartnerships, it's important to understand why doing business as usual impedes the flow of product, raises costs, and ultimately works against the goal of satisfying customer expectations.

LIFE IN THE DISTRIBUTION PIPELINE

Today's distribution pipelines generally consist of disconnected entities—organizations unable to look beyond the borders of their own operation. This myopia wastes billions of dollars every year.

Consider for a moment the role of checkout scanners—devices that could be used to fine-tune the replenishment process. Although they are used to improve labor productivity, ensure proper pricing, and generate additional revenues through sales of scanned data to third parties, they are not used in their most important and cost effective role: controlling $360 billion in product movement every year in the grocery pipeline alone, so that the right products are at the right place at the right time.

Further, decisions about how much product should be in retail stores and distribution centers are made using older and much less accurate methods. Let's revisit the scenario in the Introduction and discuss how the same products are handled through today's conventional distribution mechanisms, starting with the checkout line. We'll then compare the conventional approach with the three different distribution flows used in that scenario: direct store delivery vendors, retail DCs, and manufacturers' cross-docking facilities.

Looking for Holes

To determine what stock needs to be replenished, stores today usually assign someone the task of what I call "visual inventory review and control." This amounts to an employee walking the aisles daily and looking for "holes" in the shelves, then deciding how much to order. Normally, a hand-held device, such as a Telxon or similar piece of equipment, is used to record and transmit the ordering information to supplying locations.

The error-prone visual review process consists really of three tasks: an inventory assessment task to find and count the products; a data entry task to enter inventory data; and a forecasting task to estimate how much is needed between now and the next time the item will be reordered. While some chains recognize the importance of these tasks and make them the responsibility of a department manager, others relegate the functions to part-time people, often students, who frequently do not have the depth of knowledge about the product necessary to make informed decisions.

The good news about this approach is that regardless of the number of transaction errors, scanner data problems, or losses through theft or breakage, the aisle walker is looking at what's left. The bad news is that while most aisle walkers can be fairly accurate as inventory and data entry people, they are just not equipped to be effective forecasters. The amount of data that is needed to anticipate seasonal peaks and valleys or impact of promotions, is enormous—too greatly exceeding the ability of even the most experienced and dedicated aisle walker. As a result, the aisle walkers often over- or under-order, creating either a deficit or a surplus on the shelves or in the backroom.

In the traditional approach, the replenishment orders from the aisle walkers trigger replenishment of the inventory at the distribution center. A reorder point at the DC is typically used to order product when the on-hand balance goes below a specified number. The reorder point system uses the last several weeks of movement to calculate an average weekly or daily movement, and then assumes the future will be like the past. Based on these assumptions, the system reorders.

Rather than actual product movement in the stores, the traditional approach is based on movement out of the distribution center. When a store decides to stock up on a particular product, the usual result is that the distribution center is overstocked shortly thereafter. That's because the system's reorders are based on historical movement—in this case someone overreacting and stockpiling inventory—rather than on real movement out of the stores. The store or stores that overreacted don't place any orders for a while as they work off the excess inventory. In the meantime, the system has increased the order point at the distribution center (because it sees the increase in demand and mistakenly assumes this is a legitimate demand from customers that will continue over the next several weeks). Increasing the order point triggers an order from the manufacturer, and thus brings more product into inventory, which will then sit for some time as the stores work off their excess.

Reorder point systems fundamentally overreact—they amplify the peaks in customer demand and deepen the dips. These false alarms create overtime by overstating the marketplace demand during a peak, and create idle time by undershooting demand during a dip.

Most reorder point systems have some provision to "fool" the system. This is because the buyers realize that the future is likely to be different from the past in a number of instances. For example, before the Fourth of July, the buyer typically has to fool the system into thinking that demand for potato chips is high, to get the system to order enough to keep the stores from running out. This is a cumbersome, manual process, subject to hit-or-miss accuracy depending on when and how badly the buyer got burned in the past by running out of stock.

At the manufacturer's distribution centers, the same type of system is typically in use. At this level, the overreaction of the stores has been added to the overreaction of the distribution center to produce a demand curve that is significantly distorted. For example, the aisle walker who wanted two additional cases of tomato soup (just to be sure) caused the inventory in the distribution center to drop below the reorder point. The buyer who wanted one hundred extra cases, just to be sure, dropped the inventory in the manufacturer's distribution center below the order point. The manufacturing people in the plant reacted with dedication to their customers by scheduling overtime to resupply the distribution center. Next week, the aisle walkers realize the product is not moving, so they don't order anything. The week after that, they order less than they really need, because they remember getting chewed out by the store manager trying to find space to store the unnecessary cases they ordered two weeks earlier. There is no demand for the product from the retailer for several weeks, and now the manufacturing facility has the opposite problem—there isn't enough work to keep them busy.

Feast to famine, famine to feast—this is life in the world of reorder points.

Yet, it is all unnecessary. The data was right there in front of everyone. Historical point-of-sale data can be used to develop a forecast of demand for the item that takes into account the seasonal peaks and valleys as well as the promotions. Then last week's scanner data can be used to compare the *actual* movement to the forecast, updating the projected demand for the product. Doesn't it make sense to use this information for planning the distribution pipeline?

If the aisle walker could see that he didn't need the extra cases, he wouldn't order them. If the buyer could see the overstocking at the stores, she wouldn't reorder from the manufacturer. If the manufacturer could see the overstocking at the stores and distribution center, it wouldn't spend the money working overtime, only to have people sit on their hands a week or so later.

Keep in mind that this is how, in the grocery industry alone, *$360 billion* worth of products each year are controlled between the manufacturer's plant and the checkout scanners. There has to be a better way.

The Roving DSD Fleet

In the supermarket described in the Introduction, some types of products were replenished with astonishing speed and accuracy—Roy's soft drinks and milk, for example. That's because data was transmitted directly to store delivery vendors, who could then prepare for delivery early the next morning. In most stores today, however, whether grocery, mass merchandising, or other industries, the situation is very different: employees of the delivery vendors routinely visit the stores and check the stock on the shelves.

The DSD vendors' reps then prepare reorder forms, which must be approved by an employee of the retail store. The reps then restock the shelves.

This approach to restocking is clearly far more cumbersome than it needs to be. First, it's very labor-intensive and therefore expensive—it requires maintaining a roving fleet of shelf inspectors and restockers (one major snacks vendor maintains 11,000 DSD trucks on the road!). That's a lot of trucks and inventory! In addition to the labor costs, the approach is expensive in terms of fuel and other transportation costs.

While infopartnering may not eliminate the need for direct store suppliers to deliver to the stores, it can make their deliveries more efficient. Currently, the truck driver doesn't know what a store needs until he gets there. Fundamentally, DSD drivers are aisle walkers who happen to work for a company other than the retail chain. Like store employees, they may be fairly good at the inventory and data entry tasks, but they just cannot contain the data in their head to be effective forecasters. Consequently, they may or may not have what's needed to stock the shelves. Sometimes two stops are needed, one to assess the situation, and a second to actually restock the store. Worse, they may not have forecasted accurately and the store is out of stock by the time they visit again. The current direct store delivery approach works through the "brute force" of many visits and lots of inventory.

With an information partnership, trucks are dispatched carrying the exact quantities required for each shelf in the store, ensuring that no time or energy is wasted in visiting accounts that may not be in need of replenishment— something that happens today. The system also notifies the DSD suppliers of any stores that are predicted to be out of stock the next day so they can prevent this from happening—something that does not happen today.

In short, most stores today have not included DSD vendors in the "data loop" and miss big opportunities. In the age of infopartnering, however, DSD vendors are "wired in," so they can quickly restock shelves with the items and quantities that meet each stores' selling patterns and special needs.

Troubles in DC-Land

When Roy purchased his mayonnaise, barbecue sauce, and tomato paste, the in-store operating system recalculated the shelf inventories as soon as the items were scanned at the cash register. All three items were low, but selling at the forecasted rate, so the planning system confirmed the schedule for the item as previously calculated, to be supplied from the DC. Since the retail DCs were linked with other partners in the pipeline, such as the manufacturers, it was easy for the DC to ship the planned quantities of these items to the stores, and to maintain the appropriate levels of stock in the DC safely to handle unexpected demands.

The distribution centers typically use a reorder point to replenish their inventories. This backward-looking calculation amounts to steering the ship by looking back at its wake rather than forward at where it's going. However serious this flaw may be—as we saw earlier, it tends to aggravate the peaks in demand and overstate the dips—the reorder point approach has some other serious problems.

Reorder points don't provide a long enough horizon for the buyers and distribution people to do a good job of planning the inbound flow of product into their facilities. As a result, the DCs are not able to make the most efficient use of their resources. DCs today use an "appointment system" that schedules each truck arrival for a certain date and time. This system avoids traffic jams and empty yards, yet the very need for it underscores the fact that DCs today have limited planning capabilities. Effective planning needs to happen beyond the time frame for the appointment system. Distribution people first see the demand for resources a few days in advance. This limits their options for dealing with over- or undercapacity: they must either resort to overtime or use outside warehouse space that is already waiting.

There are other solutions to capacity problems. They include redistributing the work more evenly over the week, reducing order quantities when outside space will be needed to store products, and negotiating truck deliveries and outside storage agreements based on accurate projections. These solutions can improve the bottom line, and the quality of work life in distribution. However, they require visibility beyond the next two days.

For example, in one company the appointment system worked well to limit the number of trucks to the capacity of the facility. Unfortunately, products that were needed in the stores could not be delivered to the stores because they were waiting for an appointment. The week before, there was idle time in the facility. With greater visibility, the distribution people would have seen the underload followed by the overload and would have worked with the buyers to select some products to deliver earlier than necessary. This would have increased inventory slightly, but would have saved a considerable amount of money in the long run when compared to the overtime and out-of-stock costs that were eventually incurred.

Frequently, forecasted needs for space exceed the capacity of the DC. In such a situation, the distribution people and buyers can work together to look at any purchases that are in excess of the actual store's needs—such as position or investment buys or unnecessary safety stocks. The cost of the outside storage, additional handling, and inventory-carrying costs would then be compared to the savings from the buy. In this way, the best bottom-line solution can be chosen for the company, and since everyone is aware of the plan, there will be no surprises.

The lack of visibility also works against the manufacturers. As we've seen, the reorder point systems aggravate the peaks and dips in demand. But if the manufacturers could see the true estimate of demand, they could also use their staff and facilities more effectively. Rather than working overtime one week and then not having enough work to keep people busy the next, they could smooth the loads and operate more profitably while maintaining the same or better levels of customer service.

What if someone had your daily schedule but would only show you the next 15 minutes of your day? If this were to happen, you'd be fairly inefficient. For example, you might have to go downtown to do an errand. Later in the day you have to go to the school (also downtown) to pick up your son from soccer. Because you can't see your entire day's schedule, you end up making two trips downtown. If you could foresee your entire day, you would only make one trip—do the errand and then pick up your son, saving 40 minutes. While we all do this in our everyday life, we don't apply the same logic to the distribution of more than $1 trillion in products each year in the United States alone.

In distribution pipelines based on infopartnerships, the planning horizon extends as far out as pipeline members require. They get the visibility they need to run their operations more efficiently through the use of planning tools that can take care of manpower, equipment utilization, and storage space.

From Factory to Retail Store: The Long Cut

In some well-tuned information partnerships, data about certain items is directly transmitted to the manufacturer. The manufacturer then ships replenishment stock to a cross-docking facility, which collects bulk product from different manufacturers earmarked for the same stores. In a traditional distribution environment, the flow of information is very different. First, the retail distribution center contacts the manufacturer. The manufacturer then ships the material from a factory to a manufacturing distribution center (MDC), which in turn ships the goods to a retail distribution center (RDC). Finally, the retail distribution center ships the necessary products to the store.

Why do manufacturers and retailers both have distribution centers today? Historically, it was the only way to provide high levels of customer service. A store cannot be six days away from replenishment. Stores can't hold that much inventory, and their ability to accurately forecast their needs over that time period was low. Consequently, manufacturers set up DCs to be able to supply their retail customers on short notice, and to act as an inventory buffer to smooth the peaks and valleys in demand. Retailers set up DCs to reduce resupply time to their stores to one or two days, and to retain control over their own destiny—if it's in their warehouse, they know they can deliver it to their stores. If it's not in their warehouses, they are dependent upon the manufacturer delivering on time.

Today, it is possible to plan a schedule for each item at each store, and update the schedule every day based on the latest information. Manufacturers are capable of delivering on time, and planning their production to better meet the actual demand patterns in the marketplace. This means stores can afford to have slightly longer lead times in exchange for the significant cost savings that come from reduced handling, reduced transportation costs, and reduced inventories; they will also enjoy higher sales and profits due to fewer stockouts on the store shelves.

The driving force behind this approach, however, is the use of *information* instead of inventory to satisfy the customer's requirements. Rather than having successive levels of inventory scattered throughout the geographic area, the company uses information on the projected needs of the stores and the amount of additional stock needed in the stores to handle unexpected increases in demand. Unless stores can project their needs several days into the future, this approach to streamlining the distribution pipeline is risky. Deliveries are made to the stores every day, but they are based on projections made several days ago. The typical aisle walker is not in a position to provide forecasts that are accurate enough to use in scheduling a cross-docking facility. *The option to streamline the distribution network is only viable with an infopartnership based on effective planning.*

Even without going to a cross-docking approach, opportunities for cost savings and efficiencies exist, but most companies in distribution pipelines today can't use them because they don't have the necessary tools. For example, products in some situations can bypass distribution centers, saving both transportation and handling costs. Unfortunately, reorder point systems, which are commonly used, don't have the visibility to identify these opportunities. Skipping the manufacturer's DC or the retail DC requires an awareness of what will be shipped several days or weeks out into the future. Even if only a small percentage of all traffic can skip a level, this still can amount to significant cost savings when you account for the reduced transportation and handling costs.

In the majority of manufacturing companies, logistics people currently have their own management systems; so do manufacturing, finance, marketing, and sales. Rather than "singing from the same hymn book," most departments operate somewhat independently of one another. For example, when buyers evaluate a large purchase, they don't know whether the resulting inventory can be stored in the distribution center or whether outside storage will be required.

The "disconnect" between the systems can reach absurd proportions. In one company, during a promotion, the buyers purchased 175 vans' worth of holiday paper gift-wrap products and scheduled them for arrival on the same day. But the receiving facility only had space for 120 trucks. When the suppliers were told there was no way they could unload on the scheduled date, it set off the usual round of finger-pointing. No one wanted to accept the responsibility for a serious problem that ended up impacting the customers, because the products were not in the stores on time. Had the same schedule been used in both the buying and the distribution departments, the distribution people would have seen the capacity problem immediately, called the buyers, and worked out a solution. Customers would have been satisfied, and the departments would have worked as an effective team.

The lack of a commonly-agreed upon intradepartmental plan is not unique to retailers. Manufacturing plants tend to make what's efficient for them (which tends to be large runs) and then move it down the pipeline to distribution. "Let them figure out what to do with it" is a typical reaction, rather than viewing distribution as a customer whose schedules drive manufacturing. This often results in too much inventory in some manufacturing distribution centers and not enough in others. It even causes situations in which total inventory is up while customer service levels are down! Many of us have heard the refrain, "Our problem is not the amount of inventory we really have on hand, it's knowing *where* inventory is really needed."

If, on the other hand, an accurate schedule existed showing the demands for product, and that schedule was used to drive manufacturing's master production schedule, the entire organization would work more effectively. The different manufacturing schedules could be evaluated in terms of both manufacturing efficiency and resulting inventory. Consequently, the plan that is best for the entire company could be chosen, and there would be no surprises for either manufacturing or distribution, since they participated in developing the plan.

Hidden Capacity Constraints

Another critical difference between a distribution pipeline based on information partnerships and one based on conventional logistics is that infopartnering accounts for capacity constraints, while conventional logistics doesn't. Traditionally, capacity issues (i.e., the people, storage, equipment, and availability of raw materials needed to make the product) have been associated with manufacturing. And while capacity certainly is a major issue for manufacturing, it is a serious mistake to ignore capacity constraints in logistics, the specific hardball questions, such as, "How many trucks do I need to ship product from point A to point B?" ... "When do I need the trucks?" ... "How many people, lift trucks, and conveyor systems, and how much space do I need to unload trucks and put away product in the warehouse?" Such capacity constraints come into play at each inventory stocking location in the distribution process as goods are shipped from the factory to the factory warehouse or to the manufacturing DC, from the MDC to the wholesaler, from the wholesaler to the retail DC, and from the retail DC to the retail stores.

Current systems do nothing to show people in distribution the load that's coming to them, beyond the reservation system in terms of trucks, hours required to unload from suppliers, hours required to load for shipment to the stores, and amount of storage space required. Although the reservation system gives them some very short-term visibility—a day or two—and the orders from the stores give them a similar horizon, the system is of little value in planning these functions. The lead times for increasing man-hours, resolving conflicts when all the trucks that are needed cannot be unloaded, and so on, are longer than a few days. Buyers and distribution people need more visibility than a day or two to resolve these problems. It takes time to increase capacity in receiving and shipping, to locate additional storage, and to prioritize the most critical trucks when there is not enough capacity to handle everyone.

Ideally, the distribution people would work with the buyers on capacity problems to adjust order quantities, recalculate the real savings on a large buy (which could be less than it appears when additional storage space must be rented and additional handling must be done), and so on. These people really need to have a week or two weeks' visibility to work effectively on such problems. Without this kind of visibility, they must always have capacity in place. Sometimes the capacity will be used, but other times it will be idle, costing the company money.

In distribution pipelines owned by infopartners, the amount of space in the warehouse as well as the amount of transportation necessary are integral parts of the information flow. By the time information is sent to suppliers, all of the capacity constraints have been *taken into account*. The result is a smooth flow of product from factory to shelf. Velocity increases, too, instead of being slowed down as product wends its way through the various distribution nodes. In short, capacity constraints no longer become stumbling blocks to improved performance, because they have been recognized and managed as significant elements in the distribution process.

Other Problems: The Wholesaler/Distributor Level

Although not included in our scenario, wholesaler/distributors could also benefit enormously from participating in information partnerships. Like other types of logistics organizations today, wholesaler/distributors tend to use reorder point systems and lack integrated systems. They operate with multiple sets of numbers, and they're plagued by finger-pointing and company battles that cross departmental lines. One health and beauty care wholesale distributor operated a central distribution center which, in turn,

supported a number of satellite DCs. The buying organization was responsible for managing and controlling the level
of inventory in the central DC, and for ordering product
from suppliers to replenish the central DC. The warehouse
distribution people were responsible for controlling inventory in the satellite DCs. The two groups used different
systems, and there was a constant imbalance of product in
the pipeline—some DCs would be overflowing with tooth-
paste and deodorant while others would be short. So the
company had to maintain a constant juggling act, using
expensive and unnecessary cross-shipping between the centers to cover inventory needs. Often, the jugglers couldn't
keep up the show and let the balls drop, which meant
orders couldn't be filled.

Executives in this company were somewhat confused by
the situation, since inventory was rising while customer
service was taking a nosedive. The buyers were simply
committing product prematurely to the satellite distribution centers rather than coordinating with the warehouse
distribution people. The problem was finally solved by
implementing a planning and scheduling system that
linked the DCs together. This solution is explained in
Chapter 3.

Unfortunately, only a handful of wholesaler/distrib-
utors use time-phased resource planning and scheduling
systems. And those that operate more than a one-tier distribution network (e.g., a central supply location servicing
multiple DCs) rarely integrate the organizations with a
single set of plans. Consequently, wholesaler/distrib-
utors, like manufacturers, many times commit and deploy
inventory prematurely and inherit all the problems associated with having inventory located in the wrong place.
Further, when a consumer products manufacturer commits

product to its multiple DCs prematurely, and then discovers it has too much inventory, it often becomes "creative" and convinces the wholesaler/distributor to buy the goods. But the wholesaler/distributor doesn't have room to keep the inventory centrally, so it commits the inventory to DCs. What has really happened here is that rather than moving product to where it's needed, based on customer demand, product is pushed into locations that typically do not represent the best use of that inventory.

THE HIDDEN COSTS OF CONVENTIONAL LOGISTICS

So far, we've discussed the more obvious problems associated with operating in a distribution pipeline. Now consider this: *Logistics costs account for by far the lion's share of the costs that consumers must bear.* If the costs of logistics, marketing, sales, administration, and so on were maintained independently from the time product leaves the factories to the time it arrives in retail stores, you would find that the logistics costs exceeded all other costs by a factor of 3 to 1!

In an ideal world, there would be no logistics costs, as consumers would simply purchase their cereal, VCR, aspirin, batteries, and so on right at the factory. But in the real world, of course, that is not how goods are sold; all products have to move through a distribution pipeline until they reach a retail level. And even though their characteristics don't change as a result of their movement from factory to retail store, and no value (other than time and place) is added through the distribution process, all products incur some kind of costs for handling and transportation, ware-housing, marketing, sales, administration, etc. (see Figures 1-1A and 1-1B).

Unless all infopartners understand the breakdown of the logistics costs, it will be impossible to appreciate the magnitude of those costs and the importance of reducing them. Accountants have to rethink some of their traditional approaches so that practitioners can identify the true costs of logistics, rather than lumping them together with other business-operating expenses. The fact is, hundreds of millions of dollars are spent annually on true logistics costs in moving product into the hands of consumers. This means

FIGURE 1-1A: Logistics Cost Accumulation Within a Manufacturing Company

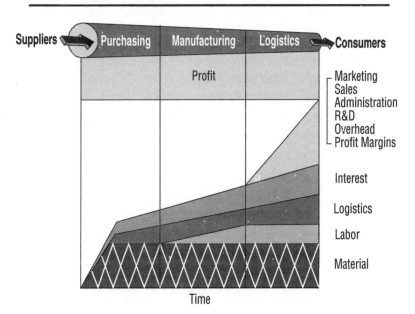

INFOPARTNERING

FIGURE 1-1B: Logistics Cost Accumulation Across the Entire Distribution Pipeline

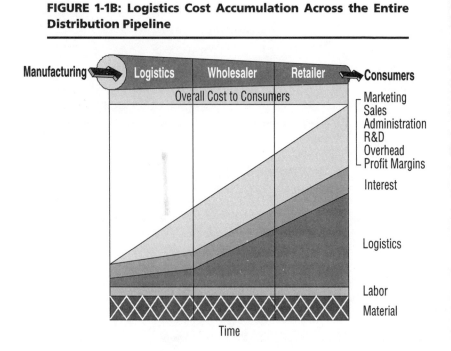

that logistics is an easy target for any company that wants to gain a competitive advantage by simplifying movement through the pipeline and cutting out accumulated costs that are normally passed on to the consumer.

CHAPTER 2

The Infopartnering Approach: Harnessing Information to Gain a Competitive Advantage

The old adage, "Information is power," rings startlingly true in business today. And as I've hinted so far, companies that harness information enjoy significantly reduced inventories, lower costs, and greatly improved customer service—all of which afford them a powerful strategic advantage over competitors that still carry on business as usual. These benefits are made possible by the following fundamental capabilities of infopartnering:

1. They integrate the entire distribution pipeline from final point of manufacture to final point of sale in a totally seamless manner.
2. They bring the complete pipeline into step with the demands of the customer, because uncertainty of de-

mand exists only at the point of final sale—not at any other point in the pipeline.

3. This then enables infopartners to deal with independent demand at store level and calculate dependent demand at all other levels in the distribution pipeline.

4. They provide a forward look into future needs, thus generating visibility through an adequate planning horizon.

5. They plan all resources (not simply product) thus ensuring a smoother flow of products from factories to store shelves.

6. This then allows companies in the distribution pipeline to effectively deal with legitimate lumps in demands (demands that vary from week to week).

7. They eliminate phony demands (demands that do not reflect true market needs). These demands exist today and unnecessarily add tremendous cost to distributed products.

In the remains of this chapter, we'll look at the lack of coordination in the pipeline and the phony demands that confuse the situation. These principles show why infopartnering achieves such spectacular results; in addition, we will look at the various types of programs that infopartners can adopt in order to coordinate their schedules and to identify the true marketplace changes in demand patterns.

BRINGING THE PIPELINE INTO STEP

In conventional distribution pipelines, uncoordinated attempts to cover uncertainty of demand with inventory at multiple levels in the pipeline are the single greatest generator of costs. Today, each pipeline member is forecasting its product needs, independent of the members above and below it in the pipeline. In addition to forecasting, each member is also estimating the uncertainty in its forecast, and planning for that in the form of safety stock. Because each pipeline member is forecasting in a vacuum, and because there have been significant peaks and valleys in the demand rates in the past, each pipeline member will carry additional inventory as a hedge against incorrect guesses. In addition, customer service may also suffer even though there may be extra inventory attempting to guard against uncertainty.

This would be the equivalent of a retailer in which each department creates its own business plan, independent of the other departments. The purchasing department makes up a forecast of what it will buy, but without any input or coordination with the sales organization. Since it knows from past experience that it will get blindsided at some point by actions that the other departments have taken, it had better put aside some money in a "surprise" account.

Similarly, top management knows it's going to open up a number of new stores, but purchasing is totally unaware of that intention. Over in distribution, people develop a plan to rent additional space and resize some areas, not realizing that this cannot work because of the increase in volume that will result from the expansion in number of stores. Distribution people also know that they often get surprised by the plans other departments have made but which they don't know about. So they too keep some money aside in a "surprise" account to deal with these unanticipated items.

When the budgets for each of the different departments are rolled up into the budget for the company, the various "surprise" accounts constitute a huge amount. This is because each department has learned—and has the scar tissue to prove it—that it should have enough in its "surprise" account to deal with the largest peak it has seen in the past. While you would never run a company this way, it is quite common for separate departments to keep one another in the dark over schedules and demand patterns in a distribution pipeline. In the same way that it makes sense for the departments in a company to work from a single set of numbers (the business plan and annual budget), it makes sense for a distribution channel to work from a single set of numbers rather than taking the "every man for himself" approach.

If this weren't bad enough, many of the surprises that each pipeline member perceives are phony. Some are real, but a good many are not. So, not only are they all covering themselves for surprises, but many of the surprises are not even genuine. In a later section, we'll look at the reasons for this. But you can see how it adds a tremendous amount of cost to the distribution pipeline.

NATURAL LINKAGES: PIPELINES LOST IN THE MIDST

To understand how infopartnerships work, it's critical to recognize that all businesses operate in some kind of a distribution pipeline, *whether they know it or not*, and whether they consider themselves collaborators, neutral partners, or even adversaries. That's because there are *natural forces* that link retailers, wholesalers, and manufacturers—what actually moves out of a retail store will ultimately impact everyone involved with the production, transportation, and sale of a product. Likewise, in some way every action that an entity in the pipeline takes will affect its fellow members.

Today, we know that information is the lifeblood of any

distribution pipeline. We also know that when pipeline members have the necessary planning and scheduling systems in place, they can share information in a way that maximizes the natural linkages that extend from manufacturer to retail store. Specifically, they can use information to tailor the flow of product so that retail stores have the right product at the right time and the right quantity; distribution organizations can move product cost-effectively; and manufacturers can make product in the most profitable and efficient manner. When natural linkages are recognized and used as building blocks, everyone involved in the pipeline wins, consumers and pipeline members alike.

Companies that take advantage of natural linkages realize the difference between actionable information and data. In business as in other aspects of life, raw data tells us very little; a mass of data from the scanner is meaningless to the rest of the pipeline unless it's tied into systems that trigger various replenishment actions throughout the pipeline. When that data are converted into specific information, pipeline members suddenly have knowledge about what product is selling, where that product is being sold, and what action is required to manufacture and distribute product.

"Real time" knowledge about product sales can be an extremely powerful tool in resynchronizing a distribution pipeline after a promotion or some other event that upsets the normal flow of goods. Back in 1958, Jay Forrester of MIT demonstrated that it could take up to six months for a factory to readjust to changes in sales patterns that occur in retail stores. Today, using infopartnering techniques that draw on natural linkages, we can slice that time down to three days! Back in the fifties—and really up until a few years ago—there were no electronic systems in use to communicate changes instantly. Data flowed manually, and it was rarely, if ever, transformed into focused information across an entire pipeline. With info-partnering, players see change immediately and can react accordingly.

DRAWING ON NATURAL LINKAGES

If natural linkages exist between businesses, why do most companies operate independently, often oblivious to, or even in spite of, each other? And if companies are bound together by natural linkages, shouldn't high levels of performance at one portion of the pipeline translate into high performance in another? Most companies operate as if they existed in a vacuum because that has been the model for "business as usual" since the early days of commercial enterprise; natural linkages do not force an awareness of interconnectedness. Moreover, they create a bridge that will guarantee that efficiencies are multiplied across an entire pipeline.

Consider the case of one mass-merchandising pipeline in which the manufacturing distribution center boasted an exemplary high level of customer service—nearly 99 percent. Oddly enough, when the retail DC owner tracked service levels at its retail outlet, which sold home electronics equipment, he was shocked to discover that the service levels were only 89 percent. How could this be? he asked. The answer: the retail store systems that triggered replenishment simply weren't up to par, they didn't provide a big enough "window" for the manufacturing DC to identify problems and take action. In other words, the manufacturing DC was doing a fine job of meeting the needs of the retail stores; the only problem was that those needs were not an accurate reflection of the needs of the customers.

Once companies realize the benefits of actively exploiting natural linkages, they can link up with complementary organizations by forging "information alliances." These alliances differ from the unilateral linkages like CRP systems that have typically been initiated by mass merchandisers or drugstore chains. Information alliances must be forged at a top executive level, because they require all organizations in the pipeline to synchronize their individual systems, to use systems that can handle legitimate lumpy demand, to do away with practices that cause false lumpy demand, and to bring about a cultural change that affects the way people do their basic work. All of this requires buy-in and a strong commitment from the executive suite.

Companies that agree to form information alliances will need to create a vision for the way business will be conducted in the future, as well as a clear understanding of the opportunities to be seized and the hurdles that must first be overcome if the vision is to be transformed into reality. "Budding" infopartners will also want to benchmark against "best-in-class" companies that already have built successful infopartnerships, so they can determine areas of strength and weakness.

HOW INFOPARTNERSHIPS TAME DEMAND UNCERTAINTY

"So, how many mousetraps will you sell this year?" This is the $64 billion question, and it applies to all companies—retailers, wholesalers, and manufacturers alike—whether they make or sell mousetraps or computer mice.

Traditionally, every organization in a distribution pipeline does its own forecasting, starting with history—the "intrinsic" factor. Not only is this unnecessary, but it leads to significant additional cost as each group tries to guess what the others are likely to do. The fact of the matter is that a forecast is only needed at one point in the distribution pipeline: the retail store. All other forecasts (exception is made for new product introductions that must be initially forecasted by manufacturers and their trading partners) are not only unnecessary but incorrect. Once you forecast the sales at the retail store, it is a simple matter to use Distribution Resource Planning (DRP, discussed later), to calculate (and recalculate) the schedule of deliveries to the stores, to the retail DC, to the wholesale DC, and to the manufacturer's DC. There is no longer any reason to forecast at the retail DC, to the wholesaler's DC, the manufacturer's DC, or the manufacturing plant.

Years ago, Joe Orlicky, a leader in the planning and scheduling field, said, "Never forecast what you can calculate." Good advice. It is faster, cheaper, and better to plug into a planning system rather than forecasting. Faster, because it's a simple matter to recalculate the schedule every day based on the latest information; few forecasts can be so responsive. Cheaper, because instead of the aisle walkers forecasting the store demand, the buyers forecasting the retail and wholesale DC level demand, and the manufacturing sales organization forecasting the plant's demand, only one forecast is needed. And better, because the planning system is based on a wealth of sales data that has become available, promotion plans, and so on. The system is also better because it is less likely to be biased.

For example, in some manufacturing companies sales and marketing people tend to "beef up" the forecasts they give operations because they don't believe that manufacturing will be able to make enough product to meet peak demands. In many organizations, the flip side also takes place, when sales and marketing "low-ball" the forecast to management, so they'll attain hero status when they hit their targets.

Of course, everyone understands the dynamics of such games, so they try to second-guess each other. As a result, it's not unusual to find four or five forecasts for the same groups of products! The bottom line is that many retail, wholesale, and manufacturing companies deal with forecasts that are far less accurate then they could be.

In reality, there's only one group that should be worried about the sales forecast: the people who sell products at the end of the pipeline. This may seem like a radical idea, and certainly one that flies against tradition, but some cutting-edge companies are tossing their old forecasting habits out the window and focusing instead on *independent* demand, rather than on *dependent* demand, which can be calculated once scanned data is collected at the retail end of the pipeline.

A number of retailers and manufacturers have created information partnerships that enable the suppliers to eliminate sales forecasting completely for their retail partners. These suppliers receive "real time" information about replenishment needs and have *no need whatsoever to forecast sales to their retail partners!* Within two to three years, many companies like these leaders will eliminate 80 percent of their need to forecast for customers, and by the year 2000 a substantial number of suppliers (wholesalers and manufacturers) will have eliminated the need for forecasting altogether.

Think about the implications of not having to forecast;

they're staggering! Consider the benefits for each type of organization in the distribution pipeline. Manufacturers today build inventories to protect against uncertainties; in other words, they build to stock. Wholesaler/distributors and retailers buy to stock in anticipation of demand, so they also protect themselves against uncertainties. Numerous studies have shown that safety stock accounts for *50 to 70 percent of inventories* in a distribution pipeline, making inventory the single largest cost accumulator once product leaves the factory. Unnecessary safety stock with all the storage and associated operating and handling costs is the number one enemy, slashing it while improving customer service becomes the number one objective.

Even so, companies perpetuate the creation of massive amounts of inventories that could easily be eliminated. For example, a large wholesaler in the Midwest spent $55 million on a state-of-the-art "mega" warehouse (1.2 million square feet), which the business press hailed for its use of ultra-efficient automation technology. Perhaps this warehouse *was* a technological wonder. But even more wondrous is the fact that companies prefer to invest in maintaining inventories than in finding ways to reduce them and improve customer service!

And a key way to reduce inventories is to eliminate the need for sales forecasting. When that happens, manufacturers will produce to customers' schedules, and the buying organizations will purchase the items that are selling. Essentially, everyone focuses on manufacturing and distributing product that's moving, as opposed to making and distributing further product as a hedge against uncertainty.

When companies join forces in an infopartnership, they can look at sales forecasting in a completely new way—one that recognizes the natural dependencies that exist between retailers, wholesaler/distributors, and manufacturers. For example, a retail store's needs can be calculated and passed on to the retail DC. Similarly, the inventory that retail DCs need to support their stores can be calculated and passed on to the wholesaler/distributor or transmitted directly to the manufacturing DC or factory. But for this to take place, each organization must continually ask the right questions. These questions comprise what I call the "universal logistics equation."

Back in the seventies, manufacturing pioneer Oliver Wight posed what he called the "universal manufacturing equation," which asks:

1. "What am I going to make?"
2. "What does it take to make it?"
3. "What do I have?"
4. "What do I have on order?"
5. "What do I have to get?"

By framing the manufacturing process in this way, companies learned what tools, information, and management processes they had to have in place to efficiently produce and meet customer demand. Those that applied the equation enjoyed outstanding results, including significant reductions in inventory and costs. The "universal logistics equation" applies the same thinking to the world of distribution, and asks:

1. "What am I going to sell?"
2. "Where will I sell it?"
3. "What do I have?"
4. "What do I have on order?"
5. "What do I have to get?"

As Figure 2-1 shows, the first question in the universal logistics equation need be answered only once across a given distribution pipeline, and that is at the point of final sale (the retail store). As each organization answers the subsequent questions, demand is calculated and communicated to the next level of the pipeline where inventory is maintained. Ultimately, the factories only make what the manufacturers' DCs need. The manufacturing DCs provide the wholesaler DCs only with what they need to replenish the retail DCs, and so on, until product reaches the retail store shelf.

For this arrangement to work, the companies in a distri-

FIGURE 2-1: The Universal Logistics Equation

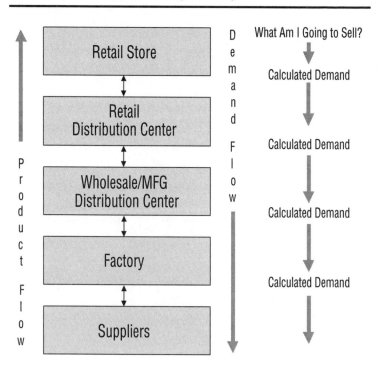

bution pipeline must each speak the same language—that is, they must use Distribution Resource Planning (DRP), Manufacturing Resource Planning (MRP II), and Just-In-Time/Total Quality Control (JIT/TQC), and share data across common lines of communication. In this way, each infopartner provides its counterparts with a tremendous amount of visibility as demand cascades from the retail store to other organizations in the pipeline.

The use of common scheduling tools also enables infopartners to simulate needs well into the future. This is especially beneficial to the manufacturing partner, which will most likely have to deal with capacity constraints and long lead times on certain key items or raw materials. By simulating a change in the pipeline, all members can see the effect, and decide what actions, if any, are appropriate. For example, what about a change in product mix? The retailer can see the different products being sold and recalculate profit margins. The distribution people can see the effects in more or less space, equipment needs, and so on. The manufacturers can see the effects in terms of changed material and capacity needs. In short, the pipeline members can go into the future with their eyes open.

DEALING WITH "LUMPS" IN THE REAL WORLD

In the real world, demand is rarely, if ever, smooth. While it would be easy to imagine a situation in which customers bought a steady 200 flea collars a week, in fact the demand on the factory will more likely be something like 1,000 flea collars this week, 50 next week, and 3,000 the following week. And not only is demand lumpy at every level in the distribution pipeline, but it changes and amplifies as it wends its way down the pipeline. What starts off as demand for 1,000 flea collars might actually end up as demand for 5,000 collars by the time it reaches the manufacturer because of various manufacturing, distribution, and financial constraints.

Let's say that a store needs twenty flea collars to meet this week's anticipated demand. Now, that store should ideally be able to get twenty collars; more likely, there are certain packaging constraints. Perhaps the supplier packages the collars in boxes of 100 each. Now the demand of 20 per week at the store has changed to 100 every five weeks. What was smooth at the customer demand level is now lumpy. The demands from all the stores in the chain are then aggregated, giving a demand for 1,200 flea collars for this week. The buyer for the chain would like to purchase 1,200 collars to meet this demand. But 3,000 collars fit on a pallet, so the demand increases to 3,000 because the buyer doesn't want to deal in half or mixed pallets. In addition, the buyer wants to ship from the factory in full truckloads.

In this case, there aren't enough pallets to fill the truck, so the buyer (or the loading software the buyer uses) selects the flea collars as the way to fill the truck. So, right away, the packaging constraints elevate the demand for 1,200 up to 6,000, unless the customer wants to spend extra money to have the product specially packaged, or handle partial or mixed pallets, which will increase handling costs. For some products, there are also manufacturer's constraints—like how often the item is produced, or minimum run sizes. As more and more manufacturing companies adopt Just-in-Time approaches, these constraints will vanish; manufacturers will be able to change over quickly from one product to another and subsequently run a mix of products that match customer requirements every single day.

The bottom line is that even a level demand for product at the stores will create demand that is lumpy as it works its way through the distribution pipeline—and few products have a level demand. Consequently, only a system that can handle lumpy demand will be effective in planning these items.

It's no longer acceptable to assume an average rate of consumption. The fact that on average you need 200 flea collars a week means little. The question is, when do you need the next case in each store, and when do you need the next pallet at the distribution center? Systems that use an average rate of consumption are unable to answer these questions accurately. Reorder point systems use an average rate of demand. They are not able to deal in terms of needing twenty this week, zero the next two weeks, twenty the week after that, and so on. For example, at the retail DC, they may keep some safety stock on flea collars, say 600. What if several stores all needed to be resupplied with flea collars in the same week? The total demand could easily be over 600, exceeding the amount of safety stock, putting the DC out of stock, and quite possibly several stores as well.

DRP systems, on the other hand, are designed to work in a time-phased format. Distribution Resource Planning (DRP) is the planning and scheduling system used to plan a distribution pipeline. DRP is a forward-looking, time-phased planning system. In a nutshell, it uses forecasts to project the inventory movement from the stores, and then calculates the replenishment schedules all the way through the pipeline, back to the manufacturing plant. Projections are made at least ten weeks into the future, and typically for a year or more. The system then reprojects these needs every day based on what actually happened.

That means that DRP systems are able to accurately calculate shipping schedules in a lumpy demand environment because the demand can be different every day. It doesn't matter whether the demand is zero, 20, 200, or 2 million in a day, the systems are designed to handle it. In the example above, a DRP system would have shown the buyer that several stores all needed replenishment in the same week (representing a total demand in that week for 800); the buyer would have, in turn, shown this demand to the manufacturer. The manufacturer would have shown the lump in demand on the correct day, and used it in its MRP II system. MRP II (Manufacturing Resource Planning) is the planning and scheduling system used to plan the manufacturing plants. MRP II takes the calculated plans from DRP (or forecasts if DRP is not in use) and uses these as the top-level demands on the plants. A master production schedule is developed using this demand data and the manufacturing capabilities. This production schedule is then converted into what materials are needed and when; and what capacities are needed and when, projecting a year or more into the future. Like DRP, these plans are recalculated frequently, typically every day, based on changes from the plan.

In the example above, the demand for 800 flea collars would have been shown in the master scheduling system, and used to develop a plan to produce enough product in a cost-efficient way to meet the demand. For example, some combination of making product earlier than needed and increasing production just prior to the lump in demand might be used at the factory. This would allow the manufacturing people to run their operation efficiently. Because everyone had visibility and could plan for the peak load in an efficient manner, things would have gone smoothly.

There would not have been a surprise out-of-stock situation, and there would not have been unnecessary costs.

With today's systems, things would have happened differently. The buyer will remember the out-of-stock situation (because few people will let them forget it), and increase the safety stock, order quantity, or both. In effect, the buyer is covering the lack of visibility with inventory. If you don't have visibility, you cannot do any load smoothing; instead, you'll have to use excess inventory, excess manpower, and excess equipment to meet the peaks and valleys in demand.

Fortunately, we've finally come to understand many of the root causes behind lumpy demand. We've also come to understand lumpy demand as a fact of business life caused by numerous quantity- and time-related factors. Examples of the quantity-related causes include lot sizes, rejects, rework, and the number of stocking locations; examples of time-related causes include promotions and deals, inventory stocking policies, seasonality, and product design changes. (See Table 2-1 for a complete listing.) (See also my book, *Distribution Resource Planning*, Oliver Wight, 1992 for more details.)

Although we can't eliminate lumpy demand, we now know that it is possible for companies participating in a distribution pipeline and infopartnering arrangements to make lumpy demand visible. Once such visibility is improved, it is possible greatly to reduce its impact on the entire pipeline. One example is the peak demand of 800 caused by several stores all ordering at the same time, as we saw above. The opposite condition is the valleys that follow the peaks. Proper planning needs to recognize both; it's equally important to know the periods when little demand will be occurring as when high demand periods will occur.

TABLE 2-1: Causes of Lumpy Demand Across the Industrial Pipeline

	Mfg.	Mfg. DCs	W/D	Ret. DCs	Retail
Quantity-Related					
Buying Lot Sizes	X	X	X	X	X
Mfg. Lot Sizes	X	X			
Packaging Lot Sizes	X	X			
Shipping Lot Sizes		X	X		X
Selling Lot Sizes			X	X	X
Stocking Lot Sizes		X	X	X	
Rejects	X				
Rework	X				
Batch Order Picking		X	X	X	
Safety Stock Changes		X	X	X	X
# Stocking Locations		X	X	X	X
Inv. Stocking Policies	X	X	X	X	X
Time-Related					
Inv. Stocking Policies	X	X	X	X	X
Seasonality		X	X	X	X
Promotions and Deals		X	X	X	X
Forward Buys			X	X	X
Diverting			X	X	X
Price Increases		X	X	X	X
End of Season Sales		X	X	X	X
Technology Improvements		X	X	X	X
Packaging Design Changes		X	X	X	X
Product Design Changes		X	X	X	X
Order Picking and Packing Time		X	X	X	X
Move Time Between Customer and Supplier		X	X	X	X
Mfg. Queue Time	X	X			
Inspection Time	X	X			
Receiving Time		X	X	X	X
Order Processing Time		X	X	X	X
Mfg. Move Time	X	X			
Mfg. Equipment Speed Time	X	X			

Mfg. = Manufacturing
Mfg. DCs = Manufacturing Distribution Centers
W / D = Wholesaler/Distributors
Ret. DCs = Retailers Distribution Centers
RETAIL = Retail Stores

André Martin, *Distribution Resource Planning.* (Essex Junction, VT: Oliver Wight Publications, 1992), p. 35.

Since everything is competing for scarce resources and we want high customer service with minimum inventories, low periods of demand become critical.

Another example is promotion. Imagine that your company has just launched a major promotional campaign for a new line of automobile tires. The promotion quickly results in a great sales uplift. The increased demand for product moves across the pipeline, creating lumpy demand. Now, in order for the companies in the pipeline to properly plan for the uplift of the promotion, it is critical to know exactly what is causing the peaks; other factors may also be contributing, such as forward buying (purchasing more than what is needed because the price is too attractive to pass up), and diverting (created by geographical deal structures). In traditional pipeline arrangements, though, it's very difficult to analyze the composition of each peak; few companies have had the necessary information or the ability to translate it.

With infopartnering, each partner in a distribution pipeline can clearly identify the composition of a peak, and plan accordingly. People can then begin to use their creativity to further dampen the effects of lumpy demand. Take promotions—with infopartnering, planned promotions at the retail level are usually passed through pipeline partners as soon as they are agreed upon. This gives the pipeline partners an enormous advantage in that they can synchronize their logistics and manufacturing schedules, adjust them where necessary, and produce and deploy products where they are needed. Tens of millions of dollars can be saved in unnecessary production and product redeployment, thus avoiding inventory excesses and shortages during and after retail promotions.

Infopartners also require several "facilitators," such as Electronic Data Interchange (EDI) and bar coding. EDI is needed to transmit the volume of data—electronic point of sale, invoices, acknowledgments, sales, on-hand balances, and inventory on order. The transmission of this kind of data in itself offers minimal benefits for most members of the distribution pipeline; the real payoff comes from marrying data transfer facilitators with systems that can create precise information as to what's needed and when it's needed—i.e., DRP and MRP II. As planning and scheduling tools for retailers, wholesalers/ distributors, and manufacturers, DRP and MRP II quickly and accurately calculate future requirements of material flow across the entire pipeline. By combining EDI with DRP and MRP II, EDI becomes a means of communicating actionable information—not just data—that will be used as the basis of future business decisions. A warning is warranted here, though: EDI cannot recognize bad data from good data, and timely efficient invalid data are worthless. Therefore, much care and attention must be devoted to avoid the data pitfall.

Bar coding facilitates communications about material flow. Multiple bar-coding applications are widely used today in the retail/wholesale, manufacturing, and transportation of products and materials. This not only eliminates errors and saves time, but is extremely efficient in identifying and tracking the movement of material from supplier to customers. Properly used as a facilitator of quick material flow, bar coding joins EDI as an ideal partner for enhancing the flow of information and material across the complete distribution pipeline.

When all infopartners have agreed to use and refine the kinds of systems just described, the pipeline in which they do business is poised for significant reductions in redundant and uncoordinated inventory, and reductions in lumpy demands that do not reflect true customer needs. This in turn leads to the enormous competitive and strategic benefits described earlier.

Infopartnerships achieve dramatic results because they break free of the practices and mind-sets that lead to unnecessarily high levels of waste and inventory. They also succeed where traditional business fails because they build on the linkages between all entities that do business with each other. In this regard, infopartnerships are like business "ecosystems"; that is, they function as an interconnected web in which each life form depends upon, and at the same supplies, other entities. Though the food chain in the business world is based on information rather than organic materials, it serves the same vital function, nourishing the entire system so that it can continue to prosper and adapt to an ever-changing environment.

CHAPTER **3**

The Heart and Soul of Infopartnering: The DRP Connection

A group of companies might have the best intentions in the world to share information with one another. But for the information to be useful, each pipeline partner must have systems in place to ensure that the right products and the right quantities can be supplied and capacity constraints are being satisfied. One without the other causes major problems.

"Now, wait a minute!", you might say. "I agree with what you said about products—that's a problem for us. But isn't capacity just an issue for manufacturers?" Certainly, production capabilities and constraints are critical to any manufacturing company. However, the same holds true for nonmanufacturers that participate in infopartnerships as well—perhaps even more so. Retailers, mass merchandisers, and wholesaler/distributors live under pressing capacity constraints, such as the number of trucks required to move product through the pipeline, or the people and handling equipment necessary for picking orders and loading trucks. Then there's the required capacity for receiving and unloading trucks, and putting product away. And how about the required capacity for space to hold inventory in distribution centers and retail stores? These are but a few of the kinds of capacity constraints that keep logistics people on their toes and define the world of pipeline distribution.

If infopartnering is to succeed, pipeline partners must equip themselves with the right tools for managing capacity constraints as they plan to move products from factories to retail stores. Chief among these tools is Distribution Resource Planning, which makes it truly possible to integrate a distribution pipeline. DRP not only focuses on what products you need and when you need them, but it takes into account your capacity constraints as it creates scheduling plans. Only by knowing your "logistical capacity" can you hope to increase product velocity.

For example, if you schedule more inventory into a distribution center than there is space, the inventory will have to be moved several times, slowing down the flow of material. The customers don't pay any more for the products because you moved them several additional times, including going to outside storage. Another example is shipping and receiving capacity. If you exceed the capacity of these resources, the flow of product will be impeded just as if a hose were pinched, creating a bottleneck ahead of the problem area. It's already been said that infopartners use information instead of inventory. Similarly, they use information instead of maintaining expensive excess capacity in other important resources like trucks, space, manpower, and equipment.

A SATELLITE'S-EYE VIEW OF DRP

DRP was developed to plan materials and capacity at every intersection of the distribution pipeline. DRP is the management process that determines the needs of products and ensures that supply sources will be able to meet the demand (see Figure 3-1). (For an in-depth description of DRP, see my book, *Distribution Resource Planning.*)

The DRP process consists of three phases. In the first, DRP receives input from a number of sources, including

1. Sales forecasts for each item in each store (not as difficult as it sounds). There would not be a forecast for the retail, wholesale, or manufacturer's DCs; DRP will calculate the shipping schedules for all of these levels based on the plan for the stores.
2. Customer orders for current and future delivery. For example, where a customer has ordered something that is not typically stocked.
3. Available inventory for sale from each inventory stocking location (ISL): the on-hand balance on the shelf and what is stored in the backroom. In the case of a DC, this would be the entire on-hand quantity, including what is stored at any outside or rented locations.
4. Incoming receipts. For stores, these could be outstanding purchase orders if this item is supplied from a DSD supplier, or in-transit amounts if this item is supplied from a distribution center. In the case of a distribution center, these would be purchase orders (retail or whole-sale DC) or distribution orders (manufacturer's DC).
5. Lead times. For stores, depending on how the item is supplied, these could be the lead time from the direct store delivery supplier or lead times from the DC. For a

FIGURE 3-1: DRP Information Flow

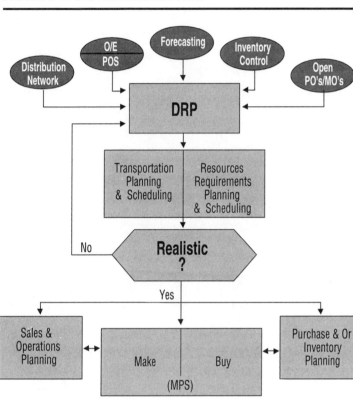

retail or wholesale DC, the lead time would be the purchasing lead time, including transportation, for a manufacturer's DC—this would typically be the transportation time from the manufacturing plant to the manufacturer's DC.

6. The mode of transport used. The mode concerns both the means of carrying the goods (typically by truck), and the deployment frequencies (or shipping schedules, as they're sometimes called).

7. Safety stock for this item at this location. Often, safety stock is assigned by class of product and stated in terms of days of supply. For example, the policy might be that all dry goods will have a two-day supply of safety stock at the DC.

8. Ordering or shipping rules. These would include the number of items in a case, the number of cases in a pallet, the weight and cube limitations of the trucks being used, and so on.

In the second phase, using all inputs mentioned above, DRP generates a "time-phased" model of the products and capacity needed to support the needs of the customer. The requirements include:

- which products are needed, how much product is needed, and when it is needed—this information is generated for each store, and each distribution center. The information is presented in the form of a schedule. For example, for Kellogg's Corn Flakes 18 oz. might show that store #125 should receive one case tomorrow, one case Friday, one case Wednesday of the following week, and so on. The schedule for a retail or a wholesale distribution center would be similar, except that the numbers would be larger, taking into account the needs of all the stores. For example, that schedule might show seventy cases needed today, eighty tomorrow, eighty the day after, sixty the day after that, and so on. Figure 3-2 is an example showing schedules for both a store and a distribution center.

- transportation capacity needed by mode of transport by ISL, as well as space needed, manpower, and equipment capacity by ISL. The transportation capacity is typically a table showing the weight and/or cube, and number of pallets between any two locations by day. The capacity planning information for transportation and space is typically represented as shown in Figures 3-3A and 3-3B.
- required inventory investment by ISL, as well as the total investment; and required level of production and/or purchases by product and supply source. These are typically shown as bar charts (see Figure 3-4).

Finally, in the third phase, DRP critiques the plans so the people can work by exception. Any time a store or DC goes below safety stock, or the required resources exceed what is

FIGURE 3-2: Store and Distribution Center Schedules

Store #125 Schedules

	Thur.	Fri.	Sat.	Sun.	Mon.	Tues.	Wed.	Thur.
Product 1	1	1	0	0	0	0	1	0
Product 2	1	0	2	0	1	0	2	0

Distribution Center Schedule

	Thur.	Fri.	Sat.	Sun.	Mon.	Tues.	Wed.	Thur.
Product 1	70	80	80	60	45	75	80	60
Product 2	65	130	65	65	65	130	65	65

FIGURE 3-3A: Transportation Plan from Manufacturer's DC to Retailer's DC

	Thur.	Fri.	Sat.	Sun.	Mon.	Tues.	Wed.
Weight	23K	28K	22K	29K	33K	23K	27K
Pallets	22	26	19	27	31	21	25

FIGURE 3-3B: Frozen Storage Space Requirements Plan

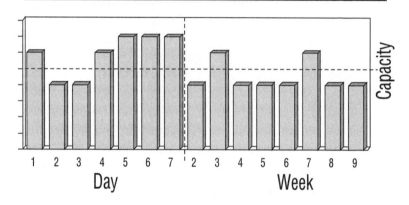

currently available, exception or action messages are generated. This way, people don't have to plow through all the data; they can go right to the problems and begin solving them. An unexpected increase in demand may require that a purchase order be expedited, or that the manufacturing department increase its master production schedule. This information is available the next day, and by exception.

DRP continually compares the timing and quantity of product on hand and on order, constantly doing the "grunt" work, the policing and critiquing of ongoing activities for its users so they can devote their attention to their

FIGURE 3-4: Required Inventory Level

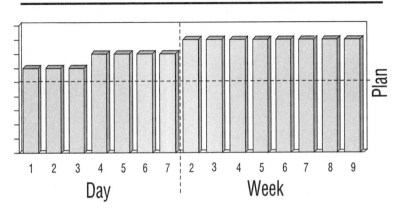

real priorities—saving the company money and boosting profits. For instance, a typical buyer might be responsible for hundreds, even thousands of items. Using DRP, he or she can set and create customized reports (e.g., "Show me all products that will run out of stock this week" . . . "Show me those products that require my taking action this week").

Without this capability of DRP, the buyer has to sort through 100 percent of the purchase orders to verify that the system is doing things correctly. In many situations, the current systems are not performing correctly because they look backward rather than forward (the buyer therefore has to look forward and "fool" the system somehow); promotions are handled outside the system; and so on. Buyers are extremely talented people, and they have an ability to save the company significant amounts of money. But they are so burdened with unnecessary clerical activities that they're only able to do effective purchasing less than 20 percent of the time. So a real strength of DRP lies in its ability to help buyers and planners truly work on an "exception" basis.

This third phase "closes the loop" between manufacturing, purchasing, logistics, and the customers. It allows the pipeline members to see what's happening using a single set of numbers. This allows them to communicate effectively in their discussions of the problem and the different options for solving it. They are able to work together as *members of a networked organization.* In so doing, DRP offers a broad range of benefits to all members of infopartnerships and the various divisions within their businesses. The general benefits to infopartners can be defined in eight significant areas.

1. *Total pipeline integration.* The schedules for the entire pipeline are calculated, and are based on previous knowledge. The schedules for the stores are calculated first. This forms the demand for the retail distribution center or DSD suppliers. All the stores supplied by a DC or all the stores supplied by a DSD branch are aggregated to give the demand for that DC or branch. DRP then calculates the schedules for these entities in the pipeline. The schedules for the DCs and DSD branches are then forwarded to the wholesalers and manufacturers as the demands on their DCs. The schedules for the DCs are calculated, and this is used to show the demand on the manufacturing plants. This aggregated demand, showing the real needs of the customers, is used to update the master production schedule so the plants are manufacturing what the customers need.

The mechanism used to transfer the schedules from stores to DCs or DSD suppliers, and from retail DCs to wholesalers' and manufacturers' DCs, and from manufacturers' DCs to the factories, is commonly called a "bill of distribution" (distribution network) (see Figure 3-5 on p. 53). A bill of distribution enables DRP users to define a distribution pipeline and show the various links between retail stores and the DCs that support them.

FIGURE 3-5: Typical Bill of Distribution (Distribution Network)

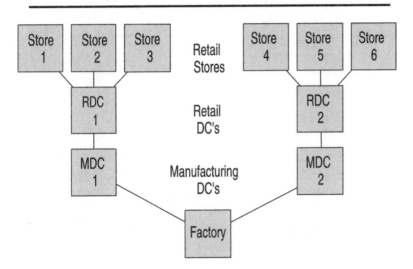

For example, if you're a retailer, you would inform DRP that your network consists of a certain number of retail stores supported by a certain number of distribution centers. If you're a wholesaler/distributor, you would define the network so that it would inform DRP of the number of distribution centers that must be scheduled. If the DCs are supported by a central supply point, then your bill of distribution would show a linkage to it. Finally, if you are a manufacturer, you would define the DCs that are supported by a given factory. In short, whether you're a retailer, wholesaler/distributor, or manufacturer, the network would be structured to carry out the required planning and scheduling so that you can interact with your pipeline partners at the highest possible level.

2. *Calculation of dependent demand.* Once a distribution pipeline has been properly defined, DRP is ready to receive sales forecasts for both baseline (normal) and

promotional requirements, and to initiate the process of planning and scheduling the entire pipeline. This allows you to eliminate forecasting everywhere except, as we discussed earlier, where it's needed—at the retail shelf level. Based on store-level sales activity, DRP calculates schedules that become dependent demand at the next level. And this is done across every level in the pipeline, determining the needs of retail stores and DCs, wholesaler/distributor DCs, and manufacturing DCs. Ultimately, it provides a set of time-phased demands that will be used to schedule the factory and supply the entire pipeline.

Notice that the retail DC, the DSD branches, the wholesale DC, the manufacturing DC, and the manufacturing plants did not have to do any redundant forecasting. In the spirit of "doing it right the first time" and "eliminating waste," the forecasting activities are done only once for the entire pipeline.

3. *Simulation of future product flows at every level in the pipeline.* One of the greatest difficulties with current retail and distribution replenishment systems is the lack of simulation capabilities. What if we open twelve new stores, what will that do to the requirements for space at the DC? What if the promotional lift is 10 percent greater than expected, will we have the product and capacity to handle it?

These are important questions in running a cost-effective, customer-focused business. Yet most executives have had to answer them with hunches or guesses, without much in the way of factual data. Because DRP is a simulation of the distribution pipeline contained within a computer, it can also be used to simulate a wide variety of other scenarios. The same information showing what product is needed and when for each stocking location, what transportation resources are needed, what space is needed, and what manpower and equipment are needed can be made available for these simulations as well as the existing plan.

4. *Resynchronizes supply and demand for the total pipeline as sales in retail stores come in higher or lower than the forecast.* The math behind DRP is very simple and straightforward; the real power of the DRP process is its ability to track ongoing activities and recalculate the plan when things happen differently from what was expected. An entire distribution network can be recalculated overnight. While the network may not be able to react that quickly, it's important to have the information on what's happening, and then as a second step, evaluate what actions to take.

For example, let's say that sales are picking up at a retail store faster than anticipated. The schedules for the stores, retail DCs, and suppliers are recalculated that night. This information is transmitted to the manufacturer, which recalculates its DC schedules and master production schedule. The next day, the master production scheduler in the plant talks with the manufacturing supervisors and purchasing people about making an adjustment to the schedule. Later that day, he has answers from both manufacturing and purchasing giving him the go-ahead. He revises the master production schedule that night; the next day, the manufacturing supervisors see revised capacity plans, and the manufacturer's suppliers see revised schedules for raw materials. A great many people talk about being focused on the customer; in this case the members of this pipeline have let their actions speak for them.

5. *Predicts the source and composition of "lumpy" demand and makes it visible across the total pipeline.* DRP is

a great "detective," making it possible easily to trace the origins of all demand. Let's say you're a buyer and you discover in week 3 of a given month that demand seems to be much higher than in the previous weeks. If, say, the normal forecast is for 100 units per week on average, and week 3 shows a forecast of 1,000 units, the buyer can trace the source of the demand and learn about its composition. The buyer can then determine whether the demand is real or the result of an error. If it's real, the buyer will have "advance" warning of the unusual "lumpiness" and can work with others in the pipeline, such as suppliers, to ensure that the demand can be supported. The net result is that lumpy demand has less negative impact on the pipeline and can be dealt with effectively.

6. *Performs warehouse receiving capacity planning.* DRP enables you to plan and simulate several days, weeks, or months into the future, telling you what should be purchased, the quantities you should purchase it in, and the dates when ordered product should arrive. This sets the stage for performing critical capacity planning actions, such as how much manpower and equipment will be needed to receive product. For example, DRP's built-in time-phasing capabilities allow users quickly to identify how many people and how much equipment will be required for a specific DC, and on which day they will be needed. This information is then compared to the DC's capacity to receive product, so that under- and over-capacity issues can be quickly identified and corrected.

Suppose a retail DC has a receiving capacity of 850 hours per day; users of DRP will identify how many receiving hours are scheduled, and they'll be able to help people quickly identify those days when there isn't enough (or there's too much) capacity to meet the incoming needs. In this way, potential bottlenecks can be identified and avoided.

7. *Performs transportation requirements capacity planning.* DRP converts the future projections of planned receipts into how many trucks will be required to ship products from point A to point B. This information is extremely useful for transportation planners; they can do a much better job of planning the utilization of their own fleet or negotiating pickups with public carriers. DRP has enabled many companies to significantly reduce transportation costs because of better planning information.

8. *Predicts warehouse space requirements and future inventory investment.* DRP is designed to convert the projected inventory investment across the planning horizon into how much space and inventory dollars are required. This information is especially useful to distribution planners. For example, if your sales were to increase by 30 percent, how much more inventory would you need, and will you have the space to hold it? The same can be done to simulate various scenarios with the previously mentioned manpower and equipment requirements. Companies that deploy DRP often use it to perform "what-if" simulations, as well, to identify potential problems and opportunities downstream.

Within the companies that enter into infopartnerships, DRP offers benefits in four key areas:

1. *Marketing and sales*—improved customer service through on-time deliveries; the ability to plan promotions more effectively; advance visibility of product availability; improved teamwork with purchasing logistics and the rest of the company.

2. *Purchasing*—better management and control of inventories, because DRP informs purchasing professionals of what to buy, when to buy it, and in what quantities to purchase it; schedules dynamically maintained to meet changing business conditions; and development of supplier partnerships through the communication of time-phased future requirements, leading to improved service and buyer productivity. In addition, DRP provides a good negotiator with the two things he or she needs in order to get the best price, delivery and quality. Having valid data and having these data extend out beyond the ordering lead times gives the negotiator excellent information and the time to do the jobs effectively.

3. *Logistics*—lower freight costs due to the reduction in rush shipments and the improved scheduling of inbound shipments; lower inventories, reduced warehouse space, reduced obsolescence through tighter control; reduced logistics costs from DCs to customers; better coordination between logistics operations and purchasing; and better budgeting. Also, it reduces the costly process of making extra shipments, that is, having shipped to Chicago, but not realizing that it's needed in the Dallas DC.

4. *Finance*—better cash-flow projections; better prediction of inventory levels; more accurate budgets; and the ability to carry out financial planning and simulations when unexpected changes within the company or marketplace occur.

Although the savings DRP offers differ by business type and industry, in general the process can affect more than 90 percent of the typical costs of distribution. That alone should be an incentive for all infopartners!

DRP IN ACTION

While relatively new to retail chains, DRP has been generating bottom-line results for the last twenty years at a number of leading-edge manufacturers and wholesaler/distributors. Let's listen to their stories—one at computer maker Digital Equipment Corporation (DEC), and the other at value-added wholesaler Mass Merchandisers, Inc. (MMI), a division of McKesson Corporation. I offer these firsthand accounts from the perspective of both an insider and an outsider—insider in that I was involved as a DRP/infopartnering consultant to both parties, outsider in that I can compare the efforts of both companies to numerous other DRP implementations, noting their striking similarities and differences.

DEC Gains a Strategic Advantage with DRP

From the standpoint of infopartnering, Digital Equipment Corporation represents an unusual case in that its pipeline consists of a large number of internal suppliers (its twenty-five factories) in addition to its hundreds, even thousands, of external suppliers. But DEC is like many other companies in that it adopted distribution resource planning out of desperation. Paul Mantos, who was DEC's senior manufacturing consultant for the Westminster, Massachusetts, distribution center during the DRP implementation, recalls that "our search for a system like DRP was literally born out of a crisis. We didn't make our earnings one quarter, because we missed the revenues by a day—the informal system couldn't keep up. So we had our own market crash. DEC's stock slipped fifty-three points. This was not only an embarrassment to management and a scare to employees, many of whom own stock in the company, but it was like the heart attack that saved the patient. We knew that we had to do something, and do it soon."

Although the impetus for finding a new formal system was accelerated by the missed numbers, the causes of the distribution problems at DEC's Westminster operation had been festering for years. As Bob Magner, the facility's distribution manager, puts it, "We used to sit and wait for the inevitable wave at the end of each quarter. We didn't know how big it was, but we knew it was coming, and couldn't take any chances. So we'd bring in an army of temporary workers to move material—at great expense, of course. Sometimes it paid off, but other times the wave wasn't as big as we expected, and a lot of the money would be wasted."

The guessing game extended to the transportation end of the business: given the uncertainties of demand, DEC couldn't tell the transportation companies exactly how many trucks it would need, because it didn't have a window into future deliveries from its internal and external suppliers. So DEC simply covered itself by requesting the maximum possible number of trucks. As business group manager Dick McGee put it, "When we went to negotiate contracts with the vendors, we were at a serious disadvantage. They knew that whatever we told them would be wrong."

In short, everyone in the pipeline suffered as a result of DEC's inability to adequately anticipate demand and plan for the smooth manufacture and movement of product. DRP changed all that, enabling the company to include distribution demand in its production planning, so that DEC's internal and external suppliers were better able to synchronize the needs of distribution with the capabilities of its factories. This ensured that all of its infopartners could drive their own manufacturing with superior information about their needs.

As a first step in implementing DRP, DEC sent several employees to a seminar to learn the basics. It then appointed one of the employees, twenty-year veteran Clem Lamarre, as program manager to head the project. Next, DEC created a steering committee that assessed the performance of each group within the distribution organization. Finally, it began a companywide educational program that led to a full-scale implementation of DRP.

While the outcome was spectacular, the implementation was not without its pain. Adopting Distribution Resource Planning, DEC discovered, was not a simple matter of teaching everyone how to use a new computer system. Rather, it represents an entirely new way of doing business, and therefore a radical change in the company's management style and culture. Now, bringing about such deep-rooted change will be difficult at any company, but DEC faced two additional challenges in making DRP a reality.

First, the company had a history of false starts on major projects (sounds familiar?). So when management first announced DRP, the effort was treated with a fair amount of skepticism. One employee recalls thinking, "Let's just wait it out—this too will pass." Not an unreasonable response, given the number of projects that had come and gone without much success.

Second, and more problematic, was the fact that DEC had traditionally given people a great deal of latitude in the way they tackled problems, but had placed little premium on their working together from a master game plan. And while a high-tech company on the leading edge of the marketplace needs to be somewhat freewheeling and allow its employees to "flex" their creativity and ingenuity, implementing DRP requires a major coordinated team effort as it crosses organizational boundaries. This cross-functional effect is typical of infopartnering projects. In the majority of cases, marketing, sales, merchandising, distribution, purchasing, etc, must be orchestrated so that they work from a master plan.

"This was extremely difficult," says Mantos. "We were a culture of expediters. We thrived on chaos and ran on an informal system. Oh, we were never out of control, though we teetered on the edge. We had a history of making diving catches in the ninth and saving the game. So the idea of planning was perceived as an intrusion, a violation of the legacy of the company."

As DEC's consultant at the time, I found the internal bickering frustrating as well as nonproductive. I had learned that the Westminster people had only one speed when it comes to getting things done: full throttle. I also recognized that DEC excelled at execution and wanted little to do with anything else. But at the same time, I realized that internal bickering and the inability to sit down for five minutes and plan threatened the entire implementation. I presented them with an ultimatum, and shortly thereafter, the project leaders planned for a companywide kickoff to be held in cafeteria. All 1,100 employees would be invited to listen to presentations by top management, myself, and their peers. This, too, was a first for Westminster, and sent a strong signal that DRP wasn't going to be just a flash in the pan; rather, it was going to be a well-coordinated undertaking that would eliminate most of the problems that caused the monthly wave of uncertainty with its sometimes disastrous effects.

DEC followed what is known as the "standard" DRP implementation path, but added a few twists of its own (such as writing its own software—not surprising for a major computer company). In addition to the required education, the company developed a number of videotapes to use as teaching tools that would enable internal staff to become trainers and coaches. For example, a planner was filmed doing her job using the new system, highlighting how that job will differ once DRP had been installed companywide. Such tapes, featuring peers rather than outside experts, served as an excellent means of communicating information and building a high comfort level. Dick McGee's group also created an ongoing communications forum called "Com 25," which consisted of "town meetings" for each of the twenty-five Westminster groups. During the meetings, anyone could voice his or her concerns and receive answers and reassurance from those at the helm.

In just two years, DEC's Westminster operation transformed itself from a reactive organization to a highly efficient player in its distribution pipeline. After the first full year of implementation, Westminster enjoyed a 55 percent increase in revenue per person, a 51 percent gain in orders per season, a 25 percent drop in the cost per order, and an impressive 37 percent overall drop in inventory.

Of course, all of these numbers translate into better customer service: 98 percent by the end of the second year. "DRP put us back in control," says Dick McGee. "Management knows it. Our employees know it. And, most important, our customers know it."

Beyond the improvements reflected in the performance numbers, Digital Equipment Corporation realized a number of qualitative benefits as well. One of the most important is a new spirit of cooperation in the Westminster operation. People learned that they could tackle a serious problem as a united team. Every manager within DEC's distribution operation believed that the lessons they learned about teamwork are just as important as the results of the DRP implementation. They no longer suffer from that most common and deadly of all corporate diseases: "functional tunnel vision."

Finally, DRP brought about remarkable culture changes at Westminster—it proved that they could work toward a common goal with a formal approach, rather than having each group fly by the seat of its pants and "reinvent the wheel" for the four hundredth time.

Each company's culture provides unique opportunities for success and unique obstacles to be overcome. In DEC's case, the energy and talent that underlies the "firefighting" culture had to be harnessed to a more orderly plan of attack. Despite the unique challenges that DEC had to face, a number of the lessons it learned are relevant for all companies that intend to participate in infopartnerships:

1. Get people involved at the highest possible level—give them a sense of ownership in the process. If DRP is "just management's project," the effort will fail.

2. Make the education as thorough as possible. And regard education primarily as an ongoing communication issue, not a one-shot event. A key indicator of the project's importance was the level of time, energy, and money committed to educating the 1,100 employees of the Westminster facility about their role in the DRP project. All told, the employees received more than 18,000 hours of education. Each person received a thorough understanding of what DRP was all about, how it would change the way they did their jobs, and how they would benefit from using it. DEC realized that education addresses the "what and why" questions, whereas training addresses the "how" questions.

3. Make sure that management's commitment to the DRP project is highly visible at all times. That means at the least signatures on all documents, a strong presence at meetings, and strong leadership by visible actions, not just talk.

The sheer size of Digital proves that it doesn't matter how big or small your operation is. If you generate enthusiasm, teamwork, and a sense of purpose, you can make programs like DRP pay off in major ways that benefit all members of the distribution pipeline.

Mass Merchandising, Inc., Forges New Path with DRP

Before 1980, Mass Merchandisers, Inc. (MMI), headquartered in Harrison, Arkansas, was using a manual vendor card system to track inventory. During the late 1970s and 1980s, MMI enjoyed rapid growth and acquired many new businesses. The company was purchased by McKesson Corporation, and assumed the information system support and inventory management functions for its sister company, Rawson Drug & Sundry. At this point, it became clear that MMI's manual system simply couldn't handle the expanded information needs. According to Bill May, a senior buyer, "Many of the buyers spent more time on the calculator than they did buying and managing inventories."

Worse, MMI was constantly out of synch with marketplace demands. Ronnie Williams, also a senior buyer, recalls, "We were basing our purchase orders on five-week sales averages, which meant seasonality could be a real problem. When the first bit of cold weather hit, for example, we knew we'd need a large quantity of cold-remedy products from the warehouse. Going out of season, we knew we'd need a lot less. But with a five-week moving average, the ordering system didn't pick on either situation, and we'd constantly find ourselves understocked or overstocked."

In the mid-1980s, MMI's top management conducted a search for a better way, and made a commitment to a complete DRP implementation. Over a two-year span, the company researched and installed new software to handle the detailed planning and scheduling needs, and conducted extensive training for all those whose jobs would be affected by the new approach to doing business. While some managers felt frustrated by the pace of the implementation, MMI wisely kept a close eye on daily operations; as a result, it did not experience any major interruptions during the process.

"We wanted to first change the purchasing tools we used to do our jobs," says executive vice president Bob Dickson. "It took longer because once we had the new tools in place, we ended up doing things operationally the way we had done them before. We finally reached a point where we knew we had reliability in the new system. The development of trust and confidence in the new system allowed us to see and believe that it would serve our needs. Once we achieved this level of trust, we could start to take advantage of DRP's full potential—that's where we are today."

MMI boasts a long list of improvements that DRP has brought about, such as a 65 percent drop in the cost of purchasing (from 1 percent of sales pre-DRP to 0.35 percent once DRP was operational). Also, in the past, when service dropped to 85 percent, it would take six weeks to recover; today, MMI offers customers near 100 percent service on key items, and using DRP's simulation capabilities, can identify and defuse potential land mines well before they disrupt service levels.

"We come in on Monday morning and DRP has prioritized our expected service-level problems," comments Steve Nelson, director of Inventory Management Systems. "It also provides us with recommendations on how to solve those problems. With this information in front of us, we can respond to fluctuations in the marketplace without compromising performance."

DRP has also enabled MMI to gain and maintain superb inventory controls. "Although we've added some ten thousand slow-moving Stock Keeping Units (SKUs) over the past four years (a thirty percent increase), our overall inventory turns have improved," Dickson explains. "A portion of our inventory today is sourced offshore, and it turns more slowly. Without DRP, the high-volume increases would have meant utter chaos."

Then there are the productivity gains that DRP affords the company. Now buyers can order an item from a vendor in three seconds. In the old days it also took about two years for buyers to become relatively productive; with DRP, buyers can become productive in as little as six to eight months. Or faster, if needs be. According to Nelson, "Today, an MMI buyer for an unfamiliar product line can manage inventories as effectively as someone who has been in it for years. For instance, in the mid-eighties, we picked up a specialty food business, which added more than five thousand items to our product list. Within six weeks, DRP enabled us to manage the inventories more effectively than we had ever been able to, even though we had no expertise with the product line."

Yet another way that the company has benefited from

DRP is the general improvement in the quality of information that each manager deals with every day. The high quality of information enables MMI's people to make plans based on what Nelson calls "scientific judgments" about the future, rather than spending their time "reacting to what was killing us yesterday."

Finally, DRP has had a significant impact on transportation operations. Since the implementation, open purchase orders are closely monitored by the freight and transportation department; this benefits all infopartners in the distribution pipeline. A key ingredient of infopartnering is the integration of the buying department's needs with the capacity and capability of the transportation and warehouse people to move, receive, and put product away. With the improved transportation scheduling that DRP affords, MMI was able to adopt a policy of paying its infopartners on the basis of hitting the DRP schedule dates, rather than on actual arrival dates. This continues to provide a great incentive for suppliers to ship on time, every time.

As impressive as the numbers may be, ask any MMI top manager about the greatest payback from DRP and you'll get the same answer, "stability" in the face of dramatic change. The company experienced dramatic growth during the late eighties, with an attendant increase in buying decisions (50 percent after assuming responsibility for Rawson's decisions—19,000 new buying decisions on top of MMI's own 36,000 annual buying decisions). Despite the new demand, MMI has maintained a consistently high level of customer service and performance.

Why does DRP work so well at MMI? Based on my observations of its implementation process, the following factors stand out and should be seriously considered by all companies engaged in infopartnerships:

1. Top management leadership and commitment, and the commitment of the necessary resources to make the DRP project succeed.
2. Top management's awareness of the need to continue routine business while implementing the new process. This sent a strong message throughout the company that DRP was a means, rather than an end itself.
3. The commitment to educate the users so they could develop the skills and develop new tools.
4. Management's acute awareness of the need for accuracy of data as a key ingredient in the DRP forecasting process.

As the experiences at DEC and MMI demonstrate, DRP is a highly effective means for planning and scheduling the acquisition of product, and the capacity to transport and receive that product throughout the distribution pipeline. Users of DRP in nonmanufacturing and manufacturing environments alike become much more productive as they become capable of anticipating problems in buying, transporting, and warehousing product. DRP becomes a common language that enables infopartners to focus on the common problems that occur across the entire pipeline. And by speaking the same language, infopartners gain their best shot at achieving and maintaining a leadership position in the marketplace.

Promotional Planning: A Major Payoff from Infopartnering

Common sense tells us that "promotions" are by definition special periods when goods are offered at reduced prices. But, as cited in *Supermarket News* (June 14, 1993, p. 13), in fact, consumer package goods companies sell as much as *40 to 70 percent* of their products to retailers during promotional periods. Based on personal experience, they sell 100 percent in certain product categories to wholesalers, as many of them only buy from deal to deal. As a rule, manufacturers promote three to four times a year, and most promotions are usually no more than three to four weeks long. In addition, store-level promotions rarely exceed one week. In the case of the grocery industry, that means $140 to $250 billion worth of product is manufactured and distributed to retail DC's roughly over a twelve-week period—about 25 percent of the available time!

The constant scramble to make product available for promotions results in costly problems for all organizations in a distribution pipeline, particularly the manufacturers. Here's why: On the average, manufacturers start making product ten to twelve weeks ahead of a promotion. Although they usually know six to eight weeks ahead that a retailer or a wholesaler/distributor will participate in the promotion, they generally won't know *how much* product will be ordered until two to three weeks before the promotion actually begins.

As a result of the lack of visibility at the end of the distribution pipeline (the retail stores and DCs), promotions often become "hit-or-miss" propositions. And given the tight timing, there is very little opportunity to redeploy inventory once a promotion has started. What's the point of having a promotion if you're likely going to face a stock-out in the middle of the allocated time frame? You'll simply wind up with frustrated customers.

At the end of a promotion, you'll also end up with excess inventory in some DCs and none in others. And when the promotion is based on special packaging (such as "25 percent more"), the unsold product must come back to the factory for repackaging—a very expensive proposition that falls on the back of the manufacturer. Ironically, although manufacturers devise the promotions, they're also the ones that get stuck with the initial inventory buildup and associated costs. But while manufacturer's take the biggest financial hit, everyone in the pipeline suffers financially when promotions are poorly executed and planned.

The further ahead you can plan a promotion, the more you can do to improve service and eliminate unnecessary production and inventories. I'm reminded of a statement made by an associate in manufacturing who once said, "Our company is the world's best at producing on overtime in anticipation of promotions, only to end up selling leftovers at distressed prices. If only we'd had a better window on what our customers really wanted, we could have doubled our profits." With infopartnering, superior information exists to completely change the way promotions are planned and executed. It's like having the opportunity to create a new set of rules in how we will manage and control the distribution pipeline.

The fact is, old rules are made to be broken, and seemingly "immutable" laws can be changed and improved. For example, you don't have to make product prematurely, then deploy it to manufacturing, wholesale, or retail DCs, and finally on to retail stores. Through infopartnering, you'll have information that will enable you to evaluate multiple deployment scenarios that postpone commitment of inventory and eliminate unnecessary handling, transportation, and warehousing across the entire distribution pipeline. In other words, it's possible to operate to a completely different set of new rules.

Infopartnering offers new rules for promotional planning and significant opportunities for greatly improving the planning and execution of promotions, which in turn results in enhanced profitability for all pipeline partners. Infopartnering improves the level-by-level visibility across the distribution pipeline, so that the manufacturing partners can synchronize production with ultimate demand and continually deploy product where it is greatly needed.

Consider how a health and beauty care retailer and manufacturer are using the power of infopartnering to plan promotions and create a "win-win" situation (see Figure 4-1). In this example, both the manufacturer and the retailer harness the power of infopartnering to create product and transport it to manufacturing and retail DCs. In this arrangement, the category managers, key account reps,

FIGURE 4-1: DRP Promotional Planning Schedule for a Health and Beauty Care Product

Today →	Week							
	1	2	3	4	5	6	7	8
Baseline	100*	120	95	--	--	40	40	35
Promotion	--	--	--	460	520	--	--	--
Total Demand	100	120	95	460	520	40	40	35
Forward Buy	--	--	--	--	350	--	--	
Grand Total	100	120	95	460	870	40	40	35

*Aggregate of all Stores for Supporting Retail DC (Numbers Shown in Case Quantities)

buyers, and members of a joint customer/supplier team plan through an eight-week horizon. As you can see in Figure 4-1, a great deal of information is available to both partners, and is transmitted electronically, using EDI and United Code Standards (UCS). Note that the information does *not* represent a DRP schedule of expected manufacturing shipments from the retail DC, nor is it a forecast of sales by the retailer to its customers. Rather, it represents a forecast of manufacturing shipments (calculated dependent demands) to the retail partner. The grand total line represents the expected shipments that the manufacturer will make during the next eight weeks.

Figure 4-1 shows that a promotion is planned for weeks 4 and 5. In addition, a forward buy order (also called "investment buy") is planned for week 5, in which the retailer will purchase quantities to be sold after the promotion. Since the manufacturer is aware of this order, it has five weeks to prepare for production and distribution of products to its retail partner. If the promotion were planned to take place during weeks 7 and 8, the manufacturer would have even more time to prepare.

What is striking in this example is the tremendous visibility available to both the retailer and the manufacturer. This window enables the manufacturer to synchronize its logistics and manufacturing resources to the needs of its retail partner and to lower costs for both, by eliminating the premature deployment of product to manufacturing DCs followed by redeployment to other MDCs as supplies run low. Customer service is also significantly improved, and product velocity to the retail DC is increased.

"Forward Commit"

Both partners in the preceding example have also deployed a new approach that I call "forward commit"—a buy order spread out several weeks into the future. Think of forward commit as a form of "bill and hold." The customer and supplier agree to a specific quantity to be purchased at a specific price. Then, a delivery schedule is agreed upon and executed. Provisions can be made in the agreement to adjust quantities at the end of the delivery schedule to account for differences between actual sales and forecasted promotion. This approach induces stability across the entire distribution pipeline and has the potential for completely eliminating large production and inventory buildups caused by forward buying and diverting (see below).

To understand how forward commit works, consider the buy order for 350 items shown in week 5 of Figure 4-1.

This order can be delivered as shown, or it can be spread out in quantities of fifty across seven weekly deliveries, starting in week 5. Other timing possibilities exist as well, either condensing or expanding the delivery schedule. The key point is that DRP, through infopartnering, makes the necessary information available, so that the partners can decide what schedule makes the most sense for them.

Forward commit allows retailers to "have their cake and eat it too"—they get the pricing benefit of a typical forward buy without having to carry the inventory. It smooths out inventory flow and greatly reduces warehousing and inventory investment costs. For the manufacturer, forward commit smooths out production and increases velocity, while reducing cost. Product is manufactured as it is needed; in essence, the system operates on "virtual inventory" that is converted into "real inventory" as it is needed.

Forward commit is a radical departure from traditional practices. It doesn't create spikes, but rather spreads out demand and brings retailers closer to being able to operate in EDLP (everyday low-price) mode. For the high/low operator, forward commit is a critical technique for smoothing out demand peaks. It enables them to enjoy the same smooth product flow of EDLP operators. In fact, with forward commit, it is almost impossible to distinguish an EDLP operator from a high/low operator. Product flow in both instances is very similar.

An exciting aspect of forward commit is that it cannot be done in a vacuum; it's a call for action for all partners across the pipeline. It doesn't matter who takes the first step, the retailer, wholesaler/distributor, or the manufacturer. All partners must be involved, must use the DRP principles and become infopartners, for the practice to work. That means greater cooperation and the potential for true integration.

STRATEGIC DEPLOYMENT: RESPONDING RAPIDLY TO CHANGE

The ability to improve promotion planning and execution across various distribution pipelines offers the single largest opportunity to remove costs from a distribution pipeline. Of course, the magnitude of the benefits will vary, depending on the intensity of capital investment in production capacity and the amount of flexibility in adjusting capacity to match demand. As a rule, capital-intensive manufacturing operations have less flexibility to significantly add or reduce production capacity without a significant financial impact.

This is why many consumer goods manufacturers must start production several weeks ahead of promotions and purposefully inventory their production capacity. In fact, they don't have a choice; therefore, very large amounts of inventories are produced ahead of needs, and these inventories cannot possibility be kept in factories after they have been made. Manufacturers must rely on past trends and historical data to predict which customers will execute their promotion, as well as in which stores, and when.

No wonder that manufacturing companies that promote brace themselves heavily for "damage control" when the promotional orders begin to roll in the door. In some companies, people are often heard making comments like, "In the heat of promotional periods, stay away from the shipping docks. The pressure is so intense out there you're likely to get shipped yourself!"

Just imagine how different the world would be if manufacturers no longer had to rely on the past to predict the future. Rather than spending a lot of time, money, and energy exercising damage control, manufacturers could work closely with their customers and jointly plan promotions at the wholesale and retail level. This new way of doing business would enable manufacturers to synchronize their resources to match the true needs of their customers. This in turn would lead to the strategic deployment of inventory and a rapid response to changes at the retail store level. Dramatic reductions in operating costs and inventories would be within reach of all pipeline partners.

INFOPARTNERING AND FORWARD BUYS

There are no readily available statistics about how much product in different industries is made and sold through forward buys, but it's safe to wager that the percentage is quite high. During my consulting career, I met many buyers who simply got into the habit of purchasing from promotion to promotion. The average time between promotions was about three months. This meant that over and above the quantities sold to consumers during promotions, significant amounts of product were purchased for normal sales between promotions. Based on these experiences, I believe that as much as *50 percent* of what is bought under the name of a promotion isn't actually sold during promotional periods.

Of course, the percentage of product in this category will vary greatly by customers and type of trade; but on average, 50 percent is probably a good "guesstimate."

With infopartnering, forward buying as currently practiced today could be completely eliminated because of the potential for using forward commit and other techniques.

If inventories are deployed professionally and the resultant savings shared equitably, they completely remove any incentives that retailers and wholesaler/distributors have to continue forward buy practices. This, in my opinion, is the key to the future of ECR.

TOP MANAGEMENT'S ROLE

If the concepts discussed in this chapter are to take hold, top managers will have to rethink many of their company's "accepted practices." Take diverting, which came into vogue immediately after the 1974 oil crisis. The crisis demonstrated to various industries that shortages—whether real or imagined—created golden opportunities to move massive amounts of product at highly inflated prices, even if the products weren't needed. By playing with pricing structures, many companies found that they could induce customers to horde product to escape announced price increases. This merely pushed product up the pipeline; the same companies would skip their orders during the next order cycle to rebalance inventories.

Marketeers in many companies then began to play games with prices, announcing a huge increase on the 1st of the following month after a quarter. This would cause an onslaught of customers and consumers who wanted to stock up before the price tag changed. To meet the increased demand, plants ran overtime in order to build up inventories. Managers would cheer on the eleventh-hour rush, since their bonuses depended on raising operating profits each quarter.

Unfortunately, when you create phony demand in the first quarter of the year, a year later if you want to show that your business is improving, you have to repeat the game just to stand still. In other words, you're stuck—which is why the pricing games continue today!

Diverting, ironically, is not only a response to the games that manufacturers play, but it enables retailers and wholesaler/distributors to exact revenge for the creation of phony demand and associated pricing. As the name suggests, "diverting" means buying a quantity of product in excess of what's needed in order to be eligible for quantity discounts, and then selling the "excess" amount to someone else. That someone else could be another retailer, wholesaler/distributor, or a divert—a broker who specializes in making diverted products available to other people.

An article in the May 10, 1993, issue of *Forbes* illustrates how the practice works:

> Say HJ Heinz ketchup regularly wholesales for 25 dollars a case. But for competitive reasons, Heinz offers a five-dollar-a-case discount to supermarket operators in Milwaukee who will buy at least 3000 cases (three truckloads).
>
> Now suppose a small grocery chain in Milwaukee needs only 1000 cases and can afford to spend only $20,000. (*Author's comment:* In the real world, the small grocery chain most likely would buy its 1000 cases from a wholesaler in Illinois playing the role of diverter.) The small grocer will put up that amount, and without broadcasting the fact to Heinz, take on a diverter as partner for the other 2000 cases of ketchup. A beautiful deal; the small grocer gets his ketchup at the same price his giant competitor pays, earns a small markup on the diverted cases, and even become eligible for the two percent discount that manufacturers typically give grocers who pay on time. A deal like that could net the grocer $2,200 in profit on a 19,600 investment, or 11.2 percent.
>
> The diverter gets cheap ketchup to sell elsewhere, buying

from a source—Heinz—that wouldn't normally sell to him. In this deal, the diverter probably nets $2 per case after shipping costs—that's a $4000 profit on a $41,000 investment, assuming a small markup to the grocery, or a 9.75 percent return on the transaction. Most diverters will do hundreds of transactions per week and earn huge returns. In some cases, employees of the manufacturers will get involved, using diverters to secretly move their products to meet quotas.*

As you can see, the diverter makes the process all the easier for the retailer and wholesaler/distributor, since no one has to go out and find a buying partner. This is great for the selling end of the pipeline, but disastrous for the manufacturer—diverting completely undermines promotional and marketing strategies. What's the point of scheduling a promotion on the East Coast when diverting will essentially create a "pseudo promotion" in the Midwest, the West Coast . . . almost everywhere else in the country? It is estimated that across the United States, $25 billion may be diverted annually!

The consumer also loses through diverting, since the exploitive practice is designed to put money in the pockets of brokers, the retailers, and wholesaler/distributors. That, of course, is not why manufacturers promote. They do so to sell more product to the consumer and also to help their retail customers create excitement in their store, which will hopefully result in increased store traffic. Since the diverted product is not actually offered to the consumer at any savings, a good deal of product that is manufactured, distributed, and sold for promotional purposes winds up be-

---

* Excerpted by permission of FORBES magazine, May 10, 1993. © Forbes Inc. 1993.

ing part of a "paper" promotion. The diverting business is exploited because it puts money in the hands of the operators, not the consumers.

In theory, at least, manufacturers won't deal with diverters, for fear of undercutting price structures and upsetting their distribution and marketing practices. Yet the practice continues in full force; some retail chains have invested significantly in warehouses and technology to facilitate diverting. "If we weren't into diverting, we'd be at a cost disadvantage," admitted Kroger spokesman Paul Burnish in the same issue of *Forbes*.

If pipeline partners are to give up diverting, they need a better mechanism for getting smaller quantities of goods. Clearly, producing unneeded product in large quantities is pure waste, and the practice increases the total cost of managing a distribution pipeline. It also ties up large amounts of unnecessary capital from factories to retail stores.

Top managers must recognize that their companies aren't in business to sit on or shift inventory—they're in business to *sell* product to the final consumer. By increasing product velocity across the entire pipeline through info-partnering, the manufacturers can share their cost savings with their retail and distribution partners, because they will be using less capital to obtain more business. This means that manufacturers can do away with pricing structures that encourage diverting practices; instead, they can afford to reward customers based on how much they sell, rather than how much they buy.

One way to measure selling performance is the economic value-added (EVA) formula, a fundamental measure of return on capital. EVA is based on the assumption that there are just three ways to increase capital: (1) earn more profit without using more capital; (2) use less working capital, such as inventory; and (3), invest capital in high-return product. EVA is tailormade for an ECR pipeline. Applied properly, it can greatly help eliminate waste and reduce total operating costs. Since the formula measures value creation and can be calculated at levels well down in the organization, it's an ideal basis for developing pricing rewards for companies, and compensation rewards for managers who help their organizations sell, rather than purchase, more product.

It's a safe bet that as long as we live in a democratic world, we'll continue to have consumer-oriented promotions in the consumer goods sector and associated trade channels. And as long as manufacturers offer discounts and price promotions, diverters will continue to exist. But this will likely change as infopartnering becomes more commonplace. At some point, managers will believe that the more we sell, the more product moves, the less capital is used (because it's not tied up in warehouses), and the more profits *everyone* in the pipeline makes. This is what infopartnering is all about and why it will ultimately revolutionize the way we plan and execute promotions.

PART II

The Infopartner's Tool Kit

CHAPTER **5**

Building a Foundation: Prerequisites and Success Factors for Infopartnering

Infopartnering represents an evolutionary jump in thinking, one based on an awareness of the potential for sharing information across companies, and using information to cut costs from an entire distribution pipeline. It not only represents the advanced application of planning and scheduling technologies capable of handling massive amounts of data very quickly and cost effectively, but reflects a radically new way of transacting business. As with any new major intracompany initiative, you can't just decide on Friday that you're going to flip a switch and surprise everyone on when they come to work on Monday. Infopartnering requires bringing about profound cultural changes, which must proceed in an orderly way, lest chaos erupts. Companies embarking on the infopartnering path must therefore prepare themselves for the changes ahead.

This chapter, based on a survey of companies currently involved with infopartnering, describes a number of key actions and mind-set changes that must take place for infopartnering to become a reality. The actions include the following:

1. *High-Level Recognition of the Opportunities.* Management at all levels must firmly believe in the potential for trimming costs from the distribution pipeline. In addition, it must believe opportunities exist to increase sales through handling demands better and managing promotions in a superior manner. Otherwise, the entire effort will become "just another program." Like quality campaigns, unless you get top-level buy-in, they won't work.

Consider Wal-Mart. When you walk into a Wal-Mart store, you'll find the same products as in other stores across the street—but at lower costs. Since the products are the same, the secret to the chain's success must lie elsewhere. In this case, it's in the way Wal-Mart has streamlined its distribution pipeline and connected with its various trading partners. Because of founder Sam Walton's relentless focus on gaining a competitive advantage—and cultivating the same goal in others within his operation—the company has been able to achieve a stunning 5 percent cost advantage over its competitors. Since profits in retailing typically run 1 to 2 percent of sales, a 5 percent cost advantage translates into a *three- to fourfold* profit advantage.

Fueled by Sam Walton's driving commitment to cutting a new path through retailing, in less than twenty-five years Wal-Mart blossomed from an obscure chain in the backwoods of Arkansas into the world's largest retailer. Although Walton didn't use the term "infopartnering," his company embraced many of the principles critical to infopartnerships, primarily those concerned with trimming fat.

Walton's commitment also bespeaks the kind of leadership required to making infopartnering successful. In addition to the fact that infopartnering requires a major cultural change and a rethinking of core business practices, it crosses traditional organizational boundaries. And any new approach to business that blurs the traditional lines between divisions will require backing from top management. Traditional boundaries also define people's "comfort zones"; when those zones are breached, people will naturally resist the change. Only top management can break down such functional barriers and resolve the kind of turf issues that inevitably surface. And only top management can change traditional objectives, reward systems, and performance measures—all of which must be adjusted for infopartnering to work.

Strong leadership is also necessary to ensure that the people in each pipeline organization receive the kind of training and building of skills they need to work differently. These skills can be acquired from outside the company, but it is always preferable to develop them internally; no one knows a company like its own people.

Finally, strong leadership is necessary to paint a broad brush stroke picture of the future. That picture should focus everyone on concepts and processes that will generate actionable information, and lay out the objectives for achieving productive relationships with pipeline partners. Top leadership should identify clearly for both employees and suppliers precisely what the infopartnership stands for and what they need to do to support it. This creates a common thread that aligns seemingly disparate functions, and provides a link between high-level strategy and the day-to-day activities that can make or break an information pipeline.

As a model for companies in the early stages of an infopartnership, top leadership should stress the following points for all employees:

A. Always keep the total distribution pipeline in mind, and constantly focus on providing better value to the consumer.

B. Strive to maintain accurate and timely information, using proven planning and scheduling systems that support effective marketing, production, and logistics decisions. This information will flow externally between partners, using EDI/UCS, ANSI, and VICS standards.

C. Focus on eliminating unnecessary inventory in all points of the pipeline, from the production line to the retail shelf.

D. Clearly identify the potential rewards of infopartnering, and promote an equitable sharing of them.

2. *Begin with the End in View.* Although an implementation plan is critical (see Chapter 9), it's equally important for those involved in the plan to have a clear sense of the ultimate goal of infopartnering. In a nutshell, this goal is the elimination of waste from the distribution pipeline so that consumers, retailers, wholesaler/distributors, and manufacturers can all profit equitably. The goal can be achieved through two means. First, by generating and sharing timely and accurate information from point-of-sale terminals at store level to point of manufacture. Second, by attaining higher product velocity across the entire pipeline, which in turn results in a continuous flow of product matched to actual consumption.

Once you see the final objective of infopartnering, return to the beginning: the use of efficient resource planning and scheduling for promotions and replenishment. Proper resource planning and scheduling is the foundation of any ECR pipeline. While it is important to become EDI-proficient and to institute bar coding, without some planning and scheduling systems, such efforts will never reach their full potential. You gain nothing just from the act of communicating electronically; inert data won't prompt action, and error-riddled, stale data will not achieve desirable results.

3. *Open People's Minds.* Many of the tasks that must be done are new to most people, since they run counter to our traditional way of thinking and doing business. That means all levels of the organization must enter an infopartnership with a new mind-set. Unfortunately, it's not so easy to change the status quo; people do not accept radical changes easily, especially when these involve the very way that they do their jobs.

For example, many people in retail organizations were trained in—and rewarded for—buying in large quantities at very low prices to take advantage of bargains, then selling some of the "excess" to other wholesalers or retailers. This might have made sense in the old days, but today it merely clogs the distribution pipeline with unnecessary inventory, ultimately elevating the cost for all partners. If retailers and others are to give up the practice of diverting, as it's called, they will have to believe that other ways of doing business are actually better. The same holds for other practices that, although commonplace in many organizations, are counterproductive from the standpoint of infopartnering.

4. *A Willingness to Accept Findings.* Numerous studies have revealed the significant potential for removing costs from distribution pipelines in industries ranging from textiles and health and beauty supplies to food and mass merchandising. Each highlights key areas where cost cutting

can take place. Those companies that have accepted the findings are poised to gain tremendous advantage in the marketplace.

The key to moving forward is to break down the "we're unique" barrier. On the surface, there seem to be innumerable formats for retail and other organizations in distribution pipelines; in reality, there are a limited number of ways to make a distribution pipeline operate efficiently. The truth is, companies that operate successful distribution pipelines and engage in infopartnerships are more alike than they are different. For example, all successful distribution pipelines will recognize the distinction between dependent and independent demand. They will all be based on effective resource planning and scheduling systems. And they will all apply the same concepts and principles across the entire distribution pipeline, from retail stores to factories. Pipeline partners will accept dependent and independent demand as facts of life, and will agree there is no need to "reengineer the wheel."

5. *Communications.* Once top management makes a commitment to participate in establishing an ECR pipeline, new lines of communication are needed. Networks of teams crossing traditional boundaries will also have to be developed, which again means that buy-in from senior management is critical. Only with the guiding of top management can teams of people from divergent organizations come together to achieve a common goal: removing cost from the pipeline.

As Jessica Lipnack, president of the Networking Institute and co-author with Jeffrey Stamps of *The TeamNet Factor* (Oliver Wight, 1993) points out, there are three basic communication issues that companies attempting to develop cross-functional teams have to consider:

1. *A clear purpose*—they must know exactly what they're
supposed to accomplish, and how they're supposed to
get there. Otherwise, lines of communication will never
function properly.

2. *Identification of members*—everyone must know their
counterparts and fellow team members. This might be as
simple as passing out a directory, but it's often neglected,
and can be the cause of many communications foulups.

3. *Build rich communication links based on trust*—the
communication links can include computer conferenc-
ing and electronic mail, as well as other technological
means of getting people "wired" together.

Finally, while infopartnering is the wave of the future, a
number of companies have already made infopartnering a
standard approach to achieving the ECR vision. *Visit them.*
Benchmarking has become an accepted means of making
quality and other improvements, and should become a standard means of developing infopartnering arrangements.
This is particularly important given the fact that there are
not—and probably never will be—any "turnkey" ECR systems. Each infopartnership will tailor commonly available
tools to its legitimate differences. A successful infopartnership is built by dedicated people, both employees and suppliers. And while outside help and guidance can be helpful,
accountability for implementing and maintaining an ECR
pipeline must ultimately rest with each infopartner.

SUCCESS FACTORS

Companies that succeed with infopartnering not only take
the prerequisites to heart, but recognize the following success factors.

1. *The Consumer Is Made Priority #1.* This might sound like a hackneyed or hollow phrase from the advertising world, but in fact, all actions on the part of a manufacturer, wholesaler/distributor, or retailer must pass the most fundamental of all business litmus tests: Does it benefit the consumer? If it doesn't, then the action is probably questionable. Let's say that someone suggests doing a promotion to sell a lot of product. On the surface, that might sound like a fine idea; after all, everyone is in business to sell. But if the end result is that it only pushes product through the pipeline and builds up inventory that sits and accumulates logistics costs, then the "victory" of the sale is pyrrhic at best; eventually the cost burden will be passed on to the consumer. By constantly questioning, infopartners can avoid wasting time, money, and energy on counterproductive actions.

2. *Unnecessary Inventory Is Considered Public Enemy #1.* If too much inventory is waste, how much inventory is needed and how much is unnecessary? You don't need a crystal ball—the *ideal amount of inventory needed* can be easily calculated. Take a look at Figure 3-5 (in Chapter 3), which represents a typical distribution pipeline for a consumer package goods company. Product moves from the factory to a manufacturing DC or a wholesale DC, then to a retail DC, and finally on to a store. In many instances, it takes an average of three days to synchronize deliveries and receive materials, one day to produce it, and two days to "QC-it." This adds up to six days in the factory.

Now, it takes an average of three days to get product from the factory to either a manufacturing DC or a wholesale DC, another three days to move it to the retail DC, and an additional day to get it to the store. Therefore, for a great many high-volume consumer package goods, the ideal amount of inventory needed across the distribution pipeline from point of manufacture to the store shelf can be a mere thirteen days (of course, this will be less for direct store delivery products).

Depending on who you read, there is anywhere from 80 to 120 days of inventory in a typical U.S. distribution pipeline. Kurt Salmon and Associates, for example, states that there is 104 days of inventory on average in its U.S. grocery sector alone. This represents more than 90 days over the ideal inventory level mentioned earlier. When you consider that $360 billion worth of product moves through this distribution pipeline every year, on average there is 100 billion worth of inventory on hand. As a result, some *$87 billion worth of unnecessary inventory* may be sitting in the U.S. grocery distribution pipeline—this is more than the combined annual sales of the top five grocery retailers in the United States! Imagine what could be done by freeing up the capital involved and its associated carrying costs.

The same phenomenon exists in all other distribution pipelines to a greater or lesser degree, whether they carry health and beauty products, consumer electronics, or office products. The opportunity to create wealth rather than waste in these industries is significant—-so significant that making unnecessary inventory public enemy number one must be among the highest priorities for any company that intends to stay in business over the long haul.

3. *Education Is a Top Priority.* If location, location, location is the key to the real estate business, then education is the key to the business of infopartnering (see Chapter 8 for in-depth coverage of the educational component). An ECR pipeline requires new knowledge—such as understanding the difference between dependent and independent demand, and applying the concept well. Companies

that want to engage in infopartnerships must provide extensive training to ensure that those skills are acquired and honed. The educational component of infopartnering must also bring about the deep cultural changes necessary to view both internal and external customers in a new light.

4. *Manufacturing Partners Take the Lead in Bringing about Change.* Manufacturers must provide retailers and wholesaler/distributors with the necessary incentives to eliminate diverting and forward buys, which create unneeded inventories across the distribution pipeline. Such inventory, pure and simple, constitutes waste. Although accountants consider inventory an asset, in the context of ECR, inventory that isn't needed is a great *liability.* It adds costs, hides problems, and masks poor management practices. Therefore manufacturers must take whatever steps they can to motivate changes in current marketing and sales practices, so that their retail and wholesale partners begin thinking in terms of efficient movement of product throughout the entire pipeline.

Retailers and wholesaler/distributors should be rewarded for how much they sell, rather than for how much they buy. The new reward incentives should be clear, concise, and easy to apply. For example, manufacturing partners need to understand that lowering prices at the end of the month to hit sales targets doesn't lead to improvements in performance; rather, it merely shifts inventory from factories or DCs to their customers' DCs.

5. *Retailers and Wholesaler/Distributors Become Active Participants.* In a few years, when we look back on successful infopartnering arrangements, we'll see completely new distribution pipelines moving products at very high velocity and quickly responding to changing consumer buying

patterns and behaviors. The biggest changes will have occurred at the retail store end of the pipeline. All products will be accurately scanned and the scanned data will drive pipeline-wide resource planning and scheduling systems. Shelf space management at store level will drive perpetual inventory control and will force the use of smaller package sizes, which will significantly reduce inventory investment on more than 50 percent of products found on most retail store shelves. Because of the availability of superior information at the retail store level, cross-docking will have become a way of life in moving products from factories to retail stores. Often, products will move directly from factory to retail stores, thus saving tens of millions of dollars for consumers and pipeline partners alike.

None of this can happen without the active participation of the retailer. Wholesaler/distributors and manufacturers cannot make the changes become reality by themselves. Historically, there's been a tendency on the part of retailers to look to wholesaler/distributors and manufacturers for improvements in profitability. While this has merit in some instances, retailers must also look inward and pursue those opportunities that will make them more efficient and generate superior information for their suppliers. In short, retailers hold the key that will open the door to the new world of infopartnering.

A new body of knowledge is emerging, based on proven concepts and principles developed in manufacturing companies and now being applied successfully in nonmanufacturing environments. This has evolved over the past twenty-five years, and the results are well documented. Resource planning and scheduling systems, such as DRP and MRP II, are today considered "universal applications."

These systems are the foundations of infopartnering and the achievement of the ECR vision.

By way of analogy, think about the accounting field. The general concepts and principles remain the same for all business and industries, regardless of the company, product, or services offered. In the same way, the world of generating information that leads to the efficient manufacture, distribution, and sale of product to the consumer has also evolved to the point where it can be applied as a standard. Now it's just a matter of more companies recognizing the potential of infopartnering and moving on to actual implementation.

CHAPTER 6

Information: The Lifeblood of ECR

It's no big news that we've entered the Information Age, and that the fundamental sources of wealth in our information economy are knowledge and communication, rather than materials, labor, and durable goods. Some experts go further, suggesting that we're in the midst of nothing less than a major business revolution driven primarily by information. Infopartnering supports the second claim, and certainly does represent a revolutionary change in the way companies conduct business and use information.

For all companies entering into ECR arrangements, the essential question is: "What information do we need to effectively manage a distribution pipeline and remove cost/waste so that we can create an advantage over our competitors?" In order to answer this question, you need to understand that there are different types of information. In this chapter, I discuss the three most important types and how they relate to each other.

THE ESSENTIAL INFORMATION TRIAD

To manage a distribution pipeline, you need three types of information: historical, which addresses "where have we been?"; factual, which focuses on "where are we now?"; and operational, which deals with the question, "where are we going?" In an infopartnership, all three types of information must eventually tie to each other, and must be timely, accurate, and complete if you are to manage the pipeline effectively. Let's consider each type in more detail.

Historical Information

To control the flow of product across a distribution pipeline, you need to know how well your company is doing—that is, how did your last sales promotion perform? Have you exceeded your sales targets? Are you improving service levels to your customers? Are your manufacturing and logistical costs within budget? Are you gaining or losing ground with your competitors; if so, against whom, how much, and in which product or category? The answers to these historical questions are all vitally important if you're going to manage your end of the distribution pipeline.

Precise and timely historical information helps you decide where to focus your resources and money to achieve your business objectives. Once you know what happened in the past, you can decide what needs fixing today. Much valuable census store scan data are available today from market research firms such as Information Resources, Inc. For a fee, they can tell you how well certain of your products are faring against a competitors', or how well your promotions performed with respect to those of your competition. The only problem is you have to sift through all the data available from external and internal sources and pick out what you really need to manage your portion of the pipeline. In a way, it's a nice problem to have.

Factual Information

Knowing what has taken place in the past, and before you can decide where to go today, you need to know where you are today. For example, once one of your promotions is over, you need to know whether you're under- or over-stocked. If so, by how much? And in which store or DC? Has the "hot" order left the supplier's factory yet? Will it arrive on time and prevent a production shutdown? Information that answers these questions falls into the factual information category.

Factual information has a certain immediacy about it; you need answers quickly and with great precision and accuracy, so that you can make the right decisions about deploying your resources. Business people need systems that deliver factual information on a continual basis, across organizational and functional boundaries. For example, you need to know whether you have enough money in the bank to cover payroll. You need to know your investment in your accounts receivables, as well as your investment in inventory. To answer these questions, you must have systems that deliver accurate and timely factual information drawn from all quarters of the company.

Operational Information

The moment you know where you've been (historical information) and where you are today (factual information), you need to figure out where you're going. Operational information that provides insights into this issue is the most important member of the Essential Info Triad.

Operational information is to an ECR pipeline as gasoline is to an automobile. Operational information ultimately enables you to manage effectively across multiple businesses, from factories to retail stores. It answers such questions as "What do we need to buy, produce, and ship to our customers?" . . . "When do we need to ship product to meet the customer's expectations?" and so on.

With operational information, you manipulate equipment, people, machines, trucks, warehouses, and other resources to get the work done and satisfy your customers. Operational information is essential for running a profitable business, because it enables you to decide how to use both the intellectual and the physical assets of your business.

As you'll learn in more detail in Chapter 7, operating systems use historical and factual information to generate information that can be used to make key decisions. That operational information must ultimately pass an important test to evaluate its quality: Does the information represent a valid simulation of your business? It's that simple. If it doesn't represent such a simulation, then it will be of dubious value in helping you make critical business decisions.

USING INFORMATION AS A SUBSTITUTE FOR INVENTORY

As we saw earlier, more than 50 percent of inventories exist as safety stock to cover for the lack of knowledge of how much inventory is needed and when that inventory must be deployed. But if you know ahead of time what your customer really wants, and that information enables you to produce product as it is needed, you can eliminate a great deal of uncertainty and begin to reduce inventories made up of safety stock. In this way, valid information about customer needs becomes a substitute for inventory.

The advent of resource planning and scheduling systems changed the way many manufacturing companies were managed in the mid-1970s. A decade later, resource planning and scheduling systems had the same impact in nonmanufacturing companies. As a result, many non-manufacturing companies today operate with significantly less inventory, largely because they've learned to replace inventory with superior operational information.

In the late seventies, when I had manufacturing responsibilities for three factories owned by Abbott Laboratories in Canada, I gained a deep respect for the power of using information as a substitute for inventory. One of the factories produced intravenous solutions in glass containers. Before we had a sound resource planning and scheduling system, we maintained, on average, a three-week supply of empty glass containers to support production. Following the implementation of MRP II, the three-week supply dropped to less than one day from April through November, and a 48-hour supply from December through March (the glass had to be brought in a day before it was used in production so that it could reach room temperature). We accomplished this feat by updating our daily time-phased production schedule once a week and sharing it with the glass supplier.

The arrangement at Abbott represents but one of the ways that companies can use superior information to replace inventory. The key is to share timely and accurate information about what product, supplies, or raw materials are needed, and when they need to be received.

During the mid-1980s, a number of wholesaler/

distributors began to understand the practice of substituting information for inventory. For example, Bowman Distribution and Mass Merchandisers, Inc., have both reduced their inventory investments 25 to 35 percent, by sharing information generated by their distribution resource planning and scheduling systems with key suppliers. Both companies refined the science and art of using systems that generate information of such high quality that it ultimately reduced the need to carry inventory. More recently, Sears has become the first retail chain to begin to reap similar benefits by applying the same concepts in the home electronics and home appliance sectors.

INFORMATION AS A SUBSTITUTE FOR BUSINESS ACTIVITIES

Sound distribution and manufacturing systems enable their users to generate information that can eliminate waste in the form of unnecessary activities across the entire distribution pipeline. For example, many companies have totally eliminated the issuing of purchase orders as well as invoices, substituting schedules instead. This is just the beginning; with a little creativity, people should be able to eliminate much of the other paperwork traditionally done to procure and pay for product.

INCOMPLETE INFORMATION DOES NOT EQUAL KNOWLEDGE

In the late 1980s, a number of companies began moving in a new direction by seeking to lower costs through what was then a radically new approach to distribution: the "continuous replenishment program" (CRP), sometimes referred to as "vendor-managed replenishment" (VMR), or "just-in-time distribution." One of the most innovative aspects of CRP/VMR is the focus on ordering a little of everything every day, and transmitting the orders electronically, rather than ordering products in larger batch sizes with buyer reviews of each order.

Another innovative aspect of CRP/VMR is the idea that retailers and/or wholesaler/distributors can provide manufacturers with their movement and inventory data, and manufacturers can manage the retailers' and/or the wholesaler/distributors' inventory, thereby reducing administrative costs in the retailing and wholesaling organizations.

Timely and accurate information is a great asset in business. But *incomplete* timely and accurate information is a great liability—especially if you don't *know* that it's incomplete. To illustrate the problems with incomplete data, let's look at the topic of continuous replenishment programs. See Figure 6-1. Most CRP programs focus on moving products from manufacturing DCs or wholesale DCs to retail DCs. Suppliers receive data—via EDI—indicating store sales, store demand, store back orders (cuts), DC on hand, and on-order inventory. This data is used by suppliers to create a sales forecast to ultimately replenish the retail DCs.

Now, from looking at the data in Figure 6-1, we could conclude that the retail DC has a two-day supply of inventory, and the supplier can take appropriate action to replenish the retail DC, depending on the lead time. The key question is, "Does the retail DC really have a two-day supply?" To answer that, we need to have more information. In other words, *the data we are working with is incomplete.*

FIGURE 6-1: Current CRP Approach

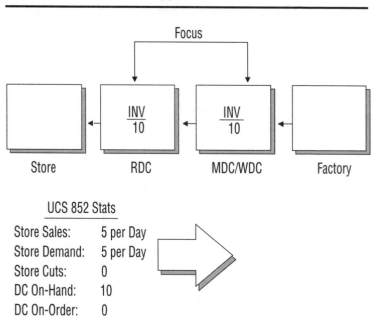

In order to have a complete picture of the information, we need to know how much inventory exists in the store. If the inventory in the store is also ten units, then it also has a two-day supply. On the other hand, if the inventory is near zero, the store needs product now. If the replenishment quantity is twenty units, the retail DC will be out of stock the moment it replenished the store. In addition, it will not have had enough inventory to satisfy the total needs of the store.

Conversely, if the store's inventory position is fifty units, then it has a ten-day supply and will not need a replenishment for a few days. In either scenario under this type of CRP approach, the supplier has no choice but to replace what is moving out of the retail DC and rely on people to compensate for the shortfall. As you can see, incomplete information—in this case caused by the lack of information about the inventory level in the retail store—can cause significant problems.

The problem is compounded depending on who is looking at the information; its inadequacies might not be apparent. The people working with the information need to have very good knowledge of how a distribution pipeline actually works. What the retail DC must have is dependent on what the store needs. So, while the store is dealing with independent demand, the demand on the retail DC can be calculated. More people need to become aware that there are two types of demand in a typical distribution pipeline, and that true independent demand only exists at the point of final sale—the retail store.

Staff who acquire the knowledge of how to manage inventory across a given distribution pipeline and can differentiate between dependent and independent demand will know immediately when they are dealing with incomplete information in a traditional CRP environment. Also, they will rely extensively on people-based systems to compensate for the lack of information until such time as the proper planning systems are implemented and network dependencies are recognized.

THE INVENTORY CAPACITY EQUILIBRIUM

Finally, we need to consider the issue of product needs and capacity needs, and how they must be equalized in a nonmanufacturing company. A few years ago, a major breakthrough occurred in manufacturing companies: We recognized that it was a total waste to do a good job of ordering materials to support an agreed-upon production schedule, only to have it arrive at the right time and the right quantity, but not have the necessary capacity available to make product. Product would arrive on time, then simply sit on the factory floor, waiting for capacity to be freed up.

Today, in many manufacturing companies, we know how to plan the needs for both material and capacity (people and equipment), to reconcile the differences, then execute the material plans and the capacity plans. The same phenomenon exists in nonmanufacturing companies, yet it largely goes unrecognized. This is unfortunate—there's no point in ordering products you need if you and your suppliers don't have the capacity to transport them (transportation capacity planning) and/or the capacity to receive and put them away (warehouse receiving capacity planning).

How often have you heard, "We were ready to ship, but there were no trucks available when we needed them"? Or, "We shipped the order on time, only to have it sit in the customer's yard for two days, waiting to be unloaded"? These sorry refrains can be heard every day in many nonmanufacturing companies. While capacity is not intentionally ignored, people are simply unused to stepping back and recognizing the importance of equalizing the need for product with the need for capacity to transport it, receive it, and put it away. As a result, we take steps to control the flow of goods in other ways. In the retail wholesale world, it's called the "appointment system" (see Chapter 1), and it evolved over time as a way of compensating for our inability to plan our receiving and transportation needs properly.

Nonmanufacturing companies need to learn from the experience of people in manufacturing environments. Systems in nonmanufacturing companies tend to be incomplete, lacking the capabilities to plan for product and capacity needs. With resource planning and scheduling, this void can be filled. And by properly planning and scheduling a distribution pipeline, product flow can be increased. Furthermore, once product and capacity needs are planned properly, suppliers receive complete information that is a true simulation of business.

INFORMATION: THE ULTIMATE ECR TOOL

To achieve the ECR vision, companies must eventually be able to answer two key questions that will ultimately control the flow of product across the entire distribution pipeline.

What will I need on the shelf?
What will I need to produce?

Retailers, wholesaler/distributors, and manufacturers that can best answer these two critical questions will have powerful information at their disposal. To answer them, you need to know what is happening in your retail stores, DCs, wholesale DCs, manufacturing DCs, and factories. You also need to know how each of the inventory stocking locations interacts and impacts one another across the entire distribution pipeline. Companies that can answer both questions in an accurate and timely fashion will know just how actual sales differ from forecasted sales, as well as the impact that the difference has on their respective operations.

Information and the Retailer

As a result of participating in an infopartnering arrangement, retailers will be able to predict the likelihood of being out of stock for each and every item. They'll also have the information that will tell them what to do to avoid stock-outs. In addition, they will know how much capacity they'll need to transport and receive product in their DCs and stores, as well as how much working capital they'll need to buy products and invest in inventory and warehouse space to efficiently manage their business.

As business conditions change, retailers in infopartner-ships will also know—dynamically and instantly—what must be done, and where, so as to react to the changes that are taking place. In other words, retailers will be able to run their businesses pro-actively, controlling the events that have the greatest impact (such as manufacturers' promotions), rather than being driven by them. In addition, they'll acquire the ability to totally simulate their business and manage it to its maximum potential, bringing to bear the full force of complete, accurate, and timely information.

Information and Wholesaler/Distributors

Some wholesaler/distributors fear the coming ECR revolution, believing that they'll be put out of business by the direct information connections between retailer and manufacturer. In fact, not only will wholesaler/distributors benefit from ECR in the same way as retailers will, but because of their strategic position in the distribution pipeline, they'll be in a unique position to use their assets (people, equipment, and warehouses) and operational information to offer exciting services to their retail and manufacturing partners. These include custom packaging and retail shelf replenishment services, cross-docking, and eliminating some of the steps that typically occur in pipelines between the time product leaves the production line and the time it's placed on store shelves.

Let's consider packaging and shelf replenishment first. Surveys have demonstrated that there is a significant opportunity to reduce inventory in retail stores—more than 50 percent of the items found on retail store shelves move less than once a week. In fact, the average inventory for those products is a three- to four-week supply. That means there's a significant opportunity for wholesaler/distributors to fill an important niche by helping manufacturers and retailers make and ship product in a completely new way. For example, manufacturers could ship product in bulk (unpacked bottles of aspirin), then have the wholesaler/distributor package the product in units tailored to a one-week supply. The wholesaler/distributor would provide a value added service, deliver the one-week supply to the retail store, and even place it on the shelves.

DRP-driven infopartnering makes such custom-packaging arrangements possible because it provides the necessary data for developing profiles for retail store sales. A profile might show, for example, that a unit consisting of six packages will nicely serve as a one-week supply for certain cluster of stores, while for another cluster, a unit of ten is more appropriate. This would be a great improvement over the current system, in which product is often packaged inappropriately for some stores; what might be a one-week supply for one is often a two-month supply for another.

Wholesaler/distributors could play a significant role in reducing inventory and freeing up valuable shelf space for other products or other uses, increasing velocity across the pipeline, and adding value to pipeline partners. I predict that some wholesaler/distributors will expand these packaging services to include transportation to stores, as well as unloading and putting product away on store shelves, so that store people don't even have to touch it. I also predict that wholesaler/distributors will use infopartnerships to work very closely with their retail and manufacturing partners in eliminating many of the steps, with their associated costs, that currently exist in moving product from the end of the production line to store shelves.

Information and Manufacturers

Information provided to manufacturers through infopartnering is like a gift that eliminates much of the costly guesswork that goes into planning inventories today. Forecasting sales will have become a thing of the past; as I've shown earlier, some companies will no longer have to forecast 80 to 90 percent of their business. To put it another way, manufacturing partners will receive their customers' dependent demands on a silver platter. When that day comes, everything a manufacturer does (and I mean *everything*) will be subject to review and change for the better.

Once uncertainty is removed from the distribution pipeline, manufacturers will be in a great position to synchronize their logistics and manufacturing resources closer to the needs of their retail and wholesaler/distribution infopartners. They will also become pro-active in servicing their customers. And as conditions change across the pipeline, manufacturing infopartners will have better information for responding to great changes in demand faster than ever before, without having to turn their logistics and manufacturing operations upside down. They will be able to support wholesaler/distributors in their custom-packaging efforts. Finally, significant costs will be avoided, an action that will greatly appeal to wholesaler/distributors.

The information provided by retailer and wholesaler/distribution partners through infopartnering will enable manufacturers to produce product and support a cross-docking requirements schedule. In many instances, product will be shipped from the end of the production line to a cross-dock location. Ultimately, one product shipment will be mixed with products from other manufacturers and shipped in full truckloads to retail stores. As a result, billions of dollars in inventory investment, material handling, transportation, and warehousing will be saved annually—and can be shared between participating infopartners. In addition, the visibility provided by the information now accessible to manufacturers will open the door to a multitude of additional opportunities for the manufacturer to reduce operating costs and improve overall business performance and productivity.

For example, a knowledge of customers' requirement schedules opens up a whole new world of opportunities for the manufacturers. Traditional approaches to managing the flow of product across a distribution pipeline provide suppliers with a view of customer requirements that extends only to the end of the ordering cycle. This is akin to having a view of your appointment calendar in half-day increments, as we said earlier. Clearly, such visibility is too short, and leads to missed opportunities to be efficient and productive.

With infopartnering, you have significantly more visibility to work with—it's like looking at your appointment calendar a week at a time. Opportunities to be more efficient and productive become quite apparent.

The info triad discussed in this chapter is a three-legged stool—you need all three legs to stand up. If you remove one leg (historical information), or even a second leg (factual information), you can still, with great acrobatic skills, manage to sit; it won't be comfortable or desirable, but you can do it. If, however, you remove the last leg, operational information, you'll wind up on the ground!

Put another way, when historical or factual information is lacking, or is inaccurate or incomplete, you can still limp along and run your business. But when operating information is lacking, you shut down production lines. DCs can't ship to stores, and you don't have product on the shelf to sell to consumers. There's simply no getting around the need for good and timely information—it's the lifeblood of the ECR pipeline.

CHAPTER **7**

Systems and Technology: The Skeleton of ECR

Ten years ago, infopartnering simply would not have been possible; we didn't have the systems necessary to transmit, receive, and process massive amounts of data across distribution pipelines, then electronically transmit the information to all trading partners. Today, all the necessary hardware and software is readily available. So the question of creating infopartnerships is not one of whether the required technology exists; rather, it's learning how we can use today's technology most efficiently and concentrate on what we need to do to participate in infopartnerships.

In the previous chapter, I discussed information as it applies to the management of the distribution pipeline. In this chapter, I turn to the systems and software needed for infopartnering to become reality—particularly, those items needed to generate the historical, factual, and operational information, the Essential Information Triad. First, though, it's necessary to discuss an issue that underlies all other information issues: scanning.

SCANNED DATA: GRIST FOR THE INFORMATION MILL

As I've stressed throughout this book, retail stores are the central nervous system of any infopartnership; success or failure of an ECR pipeline will depend on how well retailers capture information through scanners and generate the operational information that will drive the entire pipeline. Retailers must therefore consider scanned (or point-of-sale) data in a whole new light, expanding it far beyond its current use—using it for price lookups and enhancing checkout line efficiency. They must strive to ensure that checkout clerks accurately scan everything that is now scannable, and aggressively pursue ways to scan all other products that are currently keyed in manually, such as loose ballpoint pens or windshield scrapers.

There are three reasons why *all* products must be scannable:

1. Accurate, timely, and complete scanned data provides the basis for accumulating store-level past information by product.
2. Scanned data feeds the systems that ultimately generate actual information.
3. Scanned data generates inputs that are used for planning and business management purposes.

The drive to improve scanning extends beyond the retailer; manufacturers and wholesaler/distributors must work closely with their retail partners to find economical ways of making every product they sell or distribute scannable. Retail partners need to aggressively insist on that kind of involvement with their trading partners, as Wal-Mart, Kmart, and Target have done, by demanding that all products can be accurately and completely scanned. All three, for example, impose severe financial penalties on manufacturers that don't take scanning seriously, following a warning to solve problems within a specified time period. Other companies need to institute similar policies in *all* trade categories, whether they're dealing with bushels of apples, boxes of transistors, or rackfuls of sunglasses.

To ensure total point-of-sale data integrity, many retail stores will have to make significant investments in systems and training. Wal-Mart, for instance, spent $500 million on technology that enables it to tally daily sales on an item-by-item basis at all of its 2,000 stores; as a result, it has gained a significant competitive advantage. Such investments might require financial incentives from the government, but the results will be worth it; superior scanning will enable more companies to participate in infopartnerships. And infopartnering, as I've explained, is the key to prospering in the twenty-first century.

Uses of Scanned Data

Figure 7-1 shows a generic distribution pipeline comprised of a retail store and a number of inventory stocking locations (ISLs), including a retail DC, a wholesale DC, and/or a manufacturing DC. Each of these DCs has an operational infosystem that generates the information needed to run the business. The data scanned in retail stores generates information that is used to maintain perpetual inventory records for products carried on store shelves. In addition, point-of-sale data

- provides inputs for developing and maintaining historical information used for sales forecasting;

- maintains data on the "uplift" (increased sales over base-line) caused by different types of sales promotions (this information is also called "promo intelligence");
- tracks merchandise effectiveness, and monitors the execution and performance of store-level promotions (flow smoothing);
- serves as input into store-level shelf management systems; and
- provides the data needed to maintain store demographics on patterns of sales.

As Figure 7-1 shows, scanned data, after having been "cleansed," provides input into historical and factual infosystems. The cleansing process is often necessary to improve scanned data accuracy.

Figure 7-2 shows a list of the required historical, factual, and operational infosystems. Accurate, timely, and complete point-of-sale data at the retail store is essential for maintaining the historical and factual infosystems. These infosystems in turn feed the company's operational infosystems.

FIGURE 7-1: The Infopartnering Approach to Managing the Distribution Pipeline

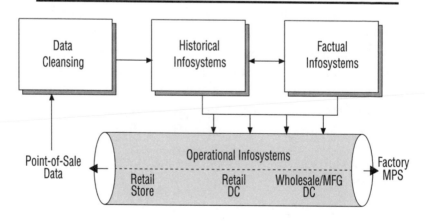

FIGURE 7-2: Required Systems for Infopartnering

Historical Infosystems	Factual Infosystems	Operational Infosystems
Point-of-Sale Transaction History	Point-of-Sale Scanning	Distribution Resource Planning & Scheduling
Promotion Intelligence History	Perpetual Inventory Control	A. Sales Forecasting
Demographics & Seasonality History	Purchase Orders	B. Computer Assisted Ordering
	Receiving	C. Transportation Capacity Planning
	Shelf Management	D. Store & Warehouse Receiving Capacity Planning
	Merchandising	
	Flow Smoothing	E. Load Building and Deployment

STORE-LEVEL HISTORICAL INFORMATION SYSTEMS

All decisions about what materials must be acquired, produced, distributed, and placed on retail store shelves begins at the store level. Consequently, retail management people must have, or develop, historical information systems that will be used to effectively manage their store operations.

Historical information becomes all the more critical when you consider that store demographics vary widely for many products. A box of twelve flashlights, or a case of forty-eight batteries, might represent a one-month supply in some stores, yet only a two-week supply or less in others. The same box of flashlights might well represent a one week or shorter supply in a specialty store during the height of the fishing or hunting season. Also, certain types of promotions are more successful than others across a wide variety of stores owned by the same retailer.

If retailers want to improve the efficiency of their store operations, and enjoy increased sales, increased inventory turns, and reduced overall costs, they must invest in the effort required to develop the information that provides the demographics and seasonality factors for every item in every store. This means that their historical infosystems must track and maintain a wide variety of information by specific retail store—including demographics, promotional intelligence, and product seasonality.

The integrity of historical data is critical if the factual and operational infosystems that depend on it are to generate valid sales forecasting and shelf management data. Well-functioning shelf management systems are particularly critical in an infopartnering environment, because they are a prerequisite (along with perpetual inventory control as discussed next) to implementing computer-assisted ordering (CAO). CAO requires that you know exactly how much shelf space the distribution resource planning and scheduling system (the key operational system in a retail store) has to manage. Unlike typical inventory management approaches, inventory management in a retail store is unique, since you have a very precise amount of shelf space to work with. And if you ignore the space constraints, you won't be able to stock your shelves with the optimal product mix.

Finally, I want to stress the importance of *store-specific* historical information. If you aspire to reaping all the benefits of CAO and, ultimately, cross-docking, you must have excellent store-specific historical information for each product. Without it, CAO and cross-docking will just be a fantasy. The good news is that if your retail operation lacks store-specific information, you're not at a competitive disadvantage—few retailers today have it either. The bad news is that in the next few years, more of your competitors will adopt it, and you *will be* at a severe strategic disadvantage if you don't develop the tools for maintaining and using historical information.

Store-Level Factual Information Systems

Once you've implemented and fine-tuned an historical infosystem, you can devote your attention to making sure that it feeds into your factual infosystems. The required store-level factual infosystems are listed in Figure 7-2. The information that these systems generate will tell you by product and by store what is on hand now, what is on order, and what is scheduled to arrive. They also show how much shelf space you must manage and replenish. In addition, they indicate the effectiveness of your various merchandising programs, and how you are performing in meeting your promotional sales objectives to consumers. As conditions change, it's vitally important to have good factual information available on a timely basis. Without it, you cannot properly manage and control sales, inventory, and the replenishment process. And when you don't have control over these areas, problems cascade across the entire distribution pipeline, severely effecting the management of retail DCs, wholesaler/distributor DCs, manufacturing DCs, and factories.

Of the factual infosystems described in Figure 7-2, perpetual inventory control is by far the most critical. Unfortunately, store-level perpetual inventory control systems have not been high on the list of priorities of the typical retailer. As a result, these control systems at the retail store level are the exception rather than the rule. Many retailers have said that it's simply an impossible task. "We have too much volume to handle and can't possibly afford to do this—the expense will exceed the benefits," has been a common excuse.

Since the early nineties, however, the cost of processing massive amounts of data at store level has dropped dramatically, so the costs are less of a factor. As a result, a small number of retailers have licked the problem of perpetual inventory control at store level, and have been able to build a solid foundation for implementing computer-assisted ordering and cross-docking. And they've demonstrated that perpetual inventory control systems are within the reach of every retail store operation.

The same can be said for shelf management systems. Most retail operations that use shelf management systems rarely extend their benefits to all their stores. Store shelf "planograms," which reveal exactly how specific items will sit on a shelf, are developed by store type, or for a certain group or cluster of stores. This, however, is not sufficient for businesses that intend to become partners in ECR pipelines. The reason is that shelf management systems generate information critical to making CAO work efficiently. In addition, they can reveal custom-packaging opportunities by showing the sales rate by store. For this to happen, however, store-shelf planograms must be *store-specific*. While many retailers agree that this is the way that shelf management systems should be used, they often cite a lack of human resources as the reason that they don't use their shelf management systems at such a finite level of detail. This constitutes an excellent opportunity for the traditional sales broker and service broker to step in and fill a void.

With a DRP-driven infopartnering pipeline, certain of the ordering activities that brokers currently have to perform will disappear. They can use the time freed up to help retail store people utilize their shelf management systems to the fullest, including servicing the shelves by working closely with wholesaler/distributors or third-party providers in cross-docking arrangements. In this way, retail sales brokers can enhance their role in the pipeline and contribute a valuable service to their retail infopartners. In the process, they'll continue to grow and prosper, as opposed to worrying (as many do now) about what will happen to them as ECR gains ground.

WHOLESALER/DISTRIBUTORS AND MANUFACTURERS: HISTORICAL/FACTUAL INFOSYSTEMS

All wholesaler/distributors and manufacturers already have, for the most part, put their historical and factual infosystems in place. As a rule, these systems do the work adequately. To bring them fully up to speed is generally not a major effort (compared to what is required to make store-level systems in retail operations "ECR-fit"). Retail DCs are also generally well served in this regard; most, if not all, retailers already have fairly good historical and factual infosystems in place in their distribution centers.

One area in which wholesaler/distributors and manufacturers could make an improvement effort is inventory record accuracy (IRA). A detailed description of the procedure for improving IRA is beyond the scope of this book; suffice it to say that inventory records in retail DCs, wholesale DCs, and manufacturing DCs must, at a minimum, be 95 percent accurate if distribution resource planning and scheduling systems are to yield useful information. Note that the 95 percent accuracy objective is not the traditional financial measure (a dollar measure); rather, it is an operational measure for people with responsibility for inventory record accuracy. (See Chapter 9 for more details. For an in-depth discussion, see Roger B. Brooks and Larry W. Wilson, *Inventory Record Accuracy: Unleashing the Power of Cycle Counting* (Oliver Wight, 1993).

OPERATIONAL INFOSYSTEMS

The ECR game will be won or lost at the operational level. First and foremost, the concepts of distribution resource planning and scheduling must be well understood and applied across the entire distribution pipeline, from retail store shelves to the doorsteps of production lines. Distribution systems used by retailers must be robust enough to forecast baseline sales and promotional sales by store and in aggregate for all stores. These systems must have the full capability of aggregating distribution demand and promotional demand to the retail DCs that service them. They must also fully support load building and deployment, as well as store and DC receiving capacity planning.

In other words, product and capacity equilibrium in nonmanufacturing environments cannot be achieved unless the operational systems in place have load building and deployment, as well as receiving capacity planning. As we saw earlier, most retailers don't have such capabilities today; as a result, their ordering systems are, in fact, really "order-launching systems" that disregard the necessary capacity to load, transport, receive, and put away product from wholesale DCs or manufacturing DCs to retail DCs.

In contrast, retail distribution resource planning and scheduling systems, when properly designed and implemented, can integrate the buying side of a retail business with the warehouse distribution and store operations side. A properly designed system can provide a valid simulation of a retail business, and the information it generates can be used to drive financial planning systems. By integrating retail operational infosystems with financial planning systems, it's possible for all the functions within a retail business to play by a common game plan.

Finally, note that the requirements described in this section also apply to wholesaler/distributors and manufacturers that operate distribution centers. To pull their weight, all the infopartners must have at their disposal the full capabilities of load building and deployment, transportation capacity planning, and warehouse receiving capacity planning. These systems will ultimately drive factory production schedules, based on robust sales forecasting capabilities, as described below.

SALES FORECASTING REVISITED

We said earlier that forecasting should ideally be done at the point of final sale, because that is the only place where independent demand truly exists. Realistically, however, it will take many years before a majority of retailers forecast at store level and begin to pass dependent demand on to others in the pipeline. Until that day comes, forecasting across the distribution pipeline will continue to be a necessity.

To become an efficient infopartner, sales forecasting systems will have to be implemented. At a minimum, these systems must have the capabilities to enable retailers to:

- develop baseline and promotional sales forecasts by retail DC, then allocate the forecast to each retail store

serviced by the RDC and carrying the product or participating in the promotion;
- represent the forecast in multiple dimensions to satisfy the needs of retail buyers, category managers, financial planners, and management; and
- display the forecast in daily, weekly, and monthly time periods, and as far out in time as is necessary (usually eight to twelve weeks in a retail setting).

In addition, overall accountability for sales forecasting in retail operations must be formalized, based on agreed-upon forecast accuracy. The same requirements apply to wholesaler/distributors and manufacturers.

COMPUTER-ASSISTED ORDERING IN RETAIL STORES

Once the retail store-level distribution system is linked to the point of sale, shelf management, perpetual inventory control, and purchase order systems, CAO can become reality in the retail store. It will replace the error-prone process of walking the aisles and conducting visual reviews, then ordering product using hand-held devices.

With DRP-driven CAO systems, retail store operations can better forecast sales (baseline and promotion), and predict how long existing inventories on the shelf (and in any backup areas) will last. The DRP/CAO system then checks to see whether anything is on order, and if so, whether it will arrive on time to avoid a possible stockout. If the answer is no, a red flag is raised for those responsible for maintaining shelf inventory. Once the planning is done, the DRP/CAO system recommends when the next order should be placed with the retail DC, with the direct store delivery vendor, with the wholesale DC, or with the manufacturing DC. In other words, the system is smart enough to know where to electronically communicate the right operational info (the calculated DRP demand) and to send it to the right supply source.

In short, the DRP/CAO system identifies future stock-outs for every product in the store, then recommends action to supply sources so that they can ship on time and in the right quantities. As sales are rung up—over or under forecast—the information is refreshed and communicated to the appropriate supply source. A key aspect of a store-level DRP/CAO system is that it generates visible, timely, and accurate operational information about what is needed in the most critical location of any distribution pipeline (the retail store shelf). It continually monitors the distribution pipeline's central nervous system, and helps answer one of the two most critical questions in managing the flow of products across the distribution pipeline: *What do I need on the shelf?* And it sets the stage for the appropriate manufacturing infopartner to answer the second most critical question: *What do I need to produce?*

HANDLING DIFFERENT CUSTOMER DEMAND STREAMS

As ECR takes hold and more companies participate in info-partnerships, wholesaler/distributors and manufacturers will need systems that can marry different types of incoming customer demand. Some customers, for example, will ask their suppliers to manage the replenishment of inventory into their DCs. For the purposes of this explanation, I'll refer to these partnering arrangements as "supplier-driven CRPs" (continuous replenishment programs). Other customers will insist on planning and forecasting their own needs and sending requirements to their suppliers—I'll call these types of partnering arrangements "customer-driven CRPs." Finally, there will be all of the other customers that will continue to do business as usual.

I would estimate that companies will have to live with these three different partnering arrangements for at least another decade. By then, the majority of customers and suppliers will be operating in a customer-driven CRP environment, greatly simplifying the process of marrying different demand streams. Until that time, wholesaler/distributors and manufacturers will need "front-end systems" for their internal systems so they can juggle the disparate streams. These front-end systems in turn must communicate with their order entry and other systems—such as transaction histories, systems that maintain data on customer sales, distribution/manufacturing resource planning and scheduling systems, and sales forecasting systems.

The wholesaler/distributor and manufacturer systems in place in most companies today were not designed to handle these different streams of customer demand. Rather, they were made to forecast, produce, distribute, and sell products in a standard way. Take sales forecasting as an example. Normally, sales forecasts are developed for all customers, then broken down into regions, territories, DC categories, and so on. With the move to ECR, sales forecasting will become customer- and location-specific. In fact, even today such targeted forecasting is already taking place. Figure 7-3 shows how a robust distribution resource planning and scheduling system can serve as a front end to develop customer-specific requirements forecasts (supplier-driven CRP), to receive requirements forecasts from customer-

FIGURE 7-3: Marrying Different Demand Streams

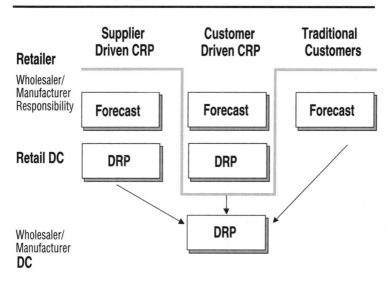

driven CRPs, and finally to generate sales forecasts from its own internal systems—and then marry them all together.

THE SEAMLESS ECR PIPELINE

A DRP/CAO system at store level lies at the heart of the information revolution described throughout this book. Imagine for a moment that you're a production scheduler in a factory 3,000 miles away from a retail store that is starting a promotion today on one of the products for which you have responsibility. Within 24 hours of the start of the promotion, it's clearly a smashing success, selling at twice the forecasted rate. In other stores within the same retail chain, it's almost the same story—they're selling on average 70 percent above the forecast. By midnight of the first day, from the start of the promotion, the DRP/CAO system has totally replanned the needs for all the stores, passed the DRP demands to the retail DC, calculated what the retail DC must ship to the stores (store replenishment), determined that the retail DC needs more product from the manufacturing DC earlier than originally planned, and electronically communicated these new needs to the manufacturing DC (refer to Figure 7-4 for the details).

The very next day, the manufacturer's DRP system replans the needs for all the manufacturing DCs, and passes

FIGURE 7-4: The Seamless ECR Pipeline

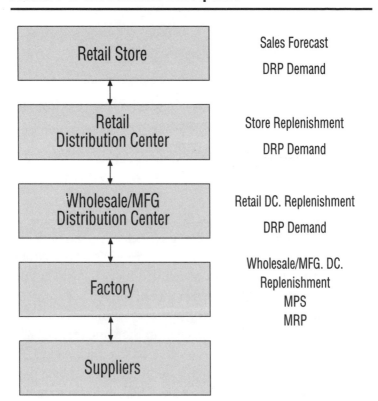

the DRP demand (wholesaler/manufacturer DC replenishment) to the factory's master production schedules. Within 48 hours of starting the promotion, everyone involved in the distribution pipeline—from the retail stores to the factory—knows exactly what is going on. They know, for example, that the promotion has started at an accelerating pace. They know exactly what to ship, how much to ship, and where to ship it in order to satisfy the increased demand.

In the preceding scenario, the production scheduler quickly receives precise information that started in specific retail stores, then passed through the retail DCs and manufacturing DCs, and made its way up through the rest of the pipeline. In short, the infopartners were totally synchronized with one another, as if they were all in the same "war room," working off of the same operational infosystem. Physical distances between the partners have been removed, providing "total pipeline visibility." As the production scheduler back at the plant, you would have gained the right information to reschedule production if necessary. And you'd do it all without a clue that the "info chain" started at a retail store 3,000 miles away!

The beauty of this approach is that you don't need to know where the demand began, unless you're troubleshooting a specific problem. If, for example, the promotion was national in scope, or covered a large region, and the same rate of success was being experienced by several retail chains in different cities, it's highly probable that the distribution resource planning and scheduling system would show DRP demand on the factory that cannot be met. In that case, you'd most likely want to know the origins of the demand—which customer, which DC, and so on. Depending on the magnitude of the demand requirements on the factory, you might make a few phone calls for a "sanity check" with the appropriate partner, to ensure that the demand is for real.

Now, the details of the scenario were fictional. But the general principles are very real—they represent infopartnering in action.

Much of the emphasis in this chapter has been placed on store operations: everything that happens in the management of the flow of goods across the pipeline begins and ends at individual retail stores. Ironically, in terms of the Essential Information Triad, the retail stores are the weakest link in the chain. If we truly aspire to take waste out of the distribution pipeline, significant investments will have to be made in systems/technologies at the store level to improve the historical and factual infosystems that feed the operational infosystems. Otherwise, the ECR vision will remain just that—a dream.

A rapid look at the most successful retailers in the United States in the past ten years will quickly demonstrate that there is a direct connection between their success rates and the degree of investment made in systems technologies. This puts the onus on top management to support the development of solid infosystems, and to ensure that all of the information generated is accurate, timely, complete, and therefore actionable. Top management must also step up to the plate and ensure that IS resources are properly focused on delivering the necessary systems, rather than just being "toys for the technicians."

The coming years will be especially critical for sales brokers, wholesaler/distributors, and manufacturers in consumer packaged goods and related trade categories.

How they implement and maintain the systems of the Essential Information Triad will largely separate out the followers from the leaders. But those that choose to follow or get out of the way should be aware that in the increasingly competitive global marketplace, they just might not get another chance to play.

CHAPTER 8

People: The Brainpower Behind ECR

Question: If you look at successful implementations, would you find more similarities than differences?

Answer: More similarities. In fact, the similarities fall into three distinct categories:

- Hardware and software
- Data integrity
- People

In typical systems implementations, the lion's share of time and money is spent on hardware and software. Top management's next concern is typically with data integrity and the scourge of the Information Age—the "GIGO" ("garbage in, garbage out") Syndrome. Sadly, the GIGO Syndrome can manifest itself in any company, and great care must be given to ensure that systems are provided with accurate, timely, and complete information (see Chapter 6 for a more in-depth exploration of this subject). Lastly, top management turns to the "people issue."

Ironically, the priorities are usually set up in reverse. Based on my observations during the last fifteen years of consulting, the degree to which a system implementation succeeds is inversely proportional to the amount of money spent on hardware, data integrity, and people. Listed below are the percentages for each of the categories:

CATEGORY	% MONEY TYPICALLY SPENT	% NEEDED FOR SUCCESS
Hardware/Software	70	10
Data Integrity	20	20
People	10	70

The fact is, once the right systems are purchased or developed in house, and once data integrity has been achieved, you're only 30 percent there; the major challenges, as you'll learn in this chapter, lie in the people area. While systems, technology, and data integrity are certainly important, success depends more on *changing the way the people do business.* That in turn means a significant reeducation effort, tearing down walls within companies, and breaking down barriers that separate companies participating in distribution pipelines.

PEOPLE VS. THE COMPUTER

When you total up the volume of data that is generated within a given distribution pipeline, retailers win the "info-prize" hands down. Retail stores generate massive volumes of data on a daily basis, and depend on systems to do their "grunt" work. The challenge, however, is to make sure that computers and systems are *adapted to the needs of people*, as opposed to the other way around. In other words, computers and systems at the retail store and DC level must help people answer routinely and daily the "universal logistics" questions:

- What am I going to sell?
- Where will I sell it?
- What do I have?
- What do I have on order?
- What do I have to get?

The bottom line is that people, not computers, are responsible—and rightly held accountable—for sales, customer service, inventory investment, and operating costs. Therefore, people must be in total control. When a store or DC goes out of stock, no one can blame the computer; it's knowledgeable people who know the products, the customers, and suppliers. And it's people who will ultimately solve business problems. Show people how to gain data integrity, and give them the necessary education and training they need, and they will generate valid information that will enable others to do their jobs in a superior way.

NEW WAYS OF DOING BUSINESS

Dealing with significant change can either prove a problem or an opportunity for people in an organization, depending on how you approach it. As a rule, people prefer the status quo—there's a natural tendency to resist change and stay within their "comfort zones." The key to removing fear of the unknown is to answer the questions that most people ask when asked to embrace a new system or process:

"What's in it for me?" . . . "For my department?" . . . "For my company?"

The questions usually come in that order—that's just how people tend to think. Most of what we do is driven by hidden agendas and assumptions rather than intentional thought. To illustrate this aspect of human nature, high-performance work system consultant Steven Rayner tells the tale of a newly married woman who cooked a ham for her husband one Easter. Her spouse noticed that she cut off the end before baking, and when he asked why, she informed him that was "simply the way it was done." The issue came up every Easter for years as a ritualistic, slightly annoying topic of conversation. One year, the woman's mother dined with the couple, and the daughter ask why the end of the ham should be sliced off before it was cooked. The mother thought for a minute, then said that Granny had always done it that way, so she assumed it was for a good reason. The pair then called Granny, who explained: "Oh, it's because my baking pan was too small to hold the whole ham."

The moral? People should never assume that *anything* is ever done for a good reason! So when giving your teams new tools, such as those used for infopartnering, it's important to help the members develop an open mind-set so that they can learn to use the tools without preconceived assumptions.

Here's an example. In most retail organizations, it's assumed that part of the buyer's job is to release a purchase order and specify its destination. Buyers typically don't have the time to converse with their own distribution people about capacity problems each time an order is placed. Even if they could, they don't have the tools to see a distribution-related capacity problem. With DRP, buyers can do the planning (in aggregate) and people in distribution can handle the execution. With DRP, you no longer have to tightly couple the ordering and the execution of the delivery. In addition, DRP gives distribution people the tools they need to identify receiving overloads, space limitations, and so on, and then work with buyers to solve the problems. In most retail and wholesale organizations today, a wide gulf separates the buyers and distribution people when it comes to solving critical capacity problems. DRP serves as a bridge, enabling the two groups of people to work in new ways—provided that they can overcome the assumption that purchase orders are necessary for doing business.

BREAKING DOWN INTRADEPARTMENTAL BARRIERS

To become effective infopartners and achieve the ECR vision, traditional organizations in retail, wholesale, and manufacturing must undergo radical changes in the next five to ten years. Specifically, they will need to create "product flow teams" (PFTs) that focus on the best way to get product from the beginning to the end of their company's segment of the distribution pipeline. To achieve higher velocity across the distribution pipeline, PFTs will require expertise in areas specific to the products for which they are responsible. Figure 8-1 shows the composition of a typical product flow team.

FIGURE 8-1: Infopartnering Product Flow Teams

Note that the focus of the product flow teams is laserlike. For example, the manufacturer's "core" team is made up of representatives from the functional areas traditionally responsible for manufacturing, distributing, and selling product. Of course other people can be added to the core team as necessary. The same concept of the core PFT applies to wholesaler/distributors and retailers, as Figure 8-1 shows.

This approach is foreign to most organizations, and may therefore cause some sweaty palms and raised eyebrows. Be assured, forming PFTs doesn't require a major "reorg"; people can still remain within their functional areas for the purposes of formal job description and payroll—think of the teams as part of a "virtual" reorganization. Even so, product flow teams must be taken very seriously if they are to lead to effective infopartnering. Top management has to provide visible support in order to bring about real changes to the authority/responsibility structure, and to ensure that team members have the opportunity to develop and implement their ideas for improvement.

Steve Rayner, in his *Recreating the Workplace: The Pathway to High Performance Work Systems* (Oliver Wight, 1993), identifies six core characteristics necessary for achieving high-performance teams. These can also be applied to the formation of PFTs:

1. Leadership that empowers others.
2. A relentless focus on strategy and results.
3. Open sharing of relevant information.
4. Borderless sharing of power.
5. A team-based design.
6. Teamwork reinforced through rewards.

A thorough discussion of these subjects is beyond the scope of this book, but it is worth looking at their underlying basis, since they are so important to the team effort essential to successful infopartnering. The following summary has been excerpted and adapted with permission from *Recreating the Workplace*:

1. *Leadership that empowers others.* Large-scale organizational change inevitably means trauma. During the change effort, some individuals will see their status, power, and position threatened, while others will be confused and frustrated as new roles and expectations are thrust upon them. Organizational change rarely happens without the emergence of one or more leaders who, through their intense convictions, serve as the sponsor, supporter, and even cheerleader for the effort. There are far too many forces maintaining the status quo for it to be disrupted without a champion for change who has a legitimate level of power and influence.

2. *A relentless focus on strategy and results.* Going to a team-based structure will accomplish little if the change is not concretely tied to an organization's overall strategic direction. In fact, PFTs must be thought of as means to an end, not ends in themselves. Managers must be very clear about the strategy they're pursuing and the results they hope to achieve to improve the performance of their business, whether these are lower costs, faster time to market, or improved customer service. Once these goals are very clear, discussion can begin on how teams may (or may not) help the organization facilitate the execution of the strategy and the attainment of the desired results.

3. *Open sharing of relevant information.* Historically, the flow of information followed a linear path upward to the privileged few. Those managers and directors lucky enough to see the figures, graphs, and charts were told by their superiors that such information was confidential.

Breakdowns of financial information, such as profit and loss statements, were almost never presented or distributed among "lower-echelon" workers. Employees typically found out about the performance of their company through the *Wall Street Journal* or the annual report. Among product flow teams, information flows like water, seeping its way into every nook and cranny in the organization. Teams absorb this information and utilize it to help in problem solving, developing innovations, and making decisions.

4. *Borderless sharing of power.* Authority, responsibility, and power should be openly shared between teams and among team members, rather than distributed among different levels of the hierarchy, based on positions and status. The clear guideline is that those most directly affected by an issue, problem, or strategy will be involved in addressing it. Management maintains the primary responsibility for setting boundary conditions—the parameters the team must work within because of budgetary, legal, timing, or strategic requirements. Well-developed boundaries provide the team with focus and increased autonomy while protecting the organization against unforeseen blunders.

5. *A team-based design.* The overall organization's design reflects an emphasis on teams as the primary work unit. Team membership is sometimes permanent, sometimes temporary, and sometimes a combination of both, depending on such things as the team's defined charter and the nature of the problem, product, or issue it is attempting to address.

6. *Teamwork reinforced through rewards.* Both formal and informal rewards reinforce the overall team-based design. There is a clear linkage between improvements made by the people and the rewards team members receive (e.g.,

profit sharing, gain sharing, etc.). A variety of methods are used to gain performance feedback at both the team and individual levels, including customer, peer, and management feedback.

The product flow team concept is the best approach I know to breaking down intracompany departmental barriers and, at the same time, providing a company with the basic internal tools it needs to become a top-notch infopartner. Once internal walls are broken down, the company can apply what it's learned to what may be the toughest hurdle of all: intercompany boundaries.

BREAKING DOWN BARRIERS BETWEEN COMPANIES

Cross-company PFTs enable a firm to sustain a competitive advantage while forming boundary-crossing relationships with competitors (through cross-docking), suppliers (through price negotiations), and customers (through shared distribution to stores). In the book referenced earlier, *The TeamNet Factor*, Jessica Lipnack and Jeffrey Stamps identify five principles that are necessary for product flow teams (or any other cross-company teams) to succeed:

1. Clarify the unifying purpose—establish the goal of the cross-company effort.
2. Identify independent members—the participants on the team.
3. Create voluntary links—provide the tools and technologies that enable people to communicate with each other (these can range from simple telephone lists to sophisticated telecommunications links).

4. Recognize the power of multiple leaders—cross-company teams will necessarily require more than one leader. This in turn demands that people think in new ways about both leading and following.
5. Stay connected at all levels—you must have a solid communication infrastructure in place for cross-company PFTs to work effectively.

Firms that apply these principles and develop effective cross-company product flow teams will be on the cutting edge of infopartnering—and will reap the associated rewards.

NEW RESPONSIBILITIES IN RETAILING

Once organizations begin to trust each other, and tools such as DRP have become a reality across the distribution pipeline, all the infopartners have a multitude of opportunities to redefine and clarify their responsibilities in many areas. Take the retail buyer. With a formal system like DRP, it becomes a practical matter to put the warehousing distribution people in direct contact with the supplier. These people can then act as supplier schedulers, who directly communicate with people at the supplier's location. With this arrangement, buyers can have the time to do the important parts of their job: sourcing, negotiating, contracting, value analysis, and so on.

In an infopartnering environment, there can be a business arrangement called the "supplier agreement" between the customer and the supplier. The supplier scheduler enters the picture after the supplier agreement is finalized. His or her job is to operate DRP and provide the suppliers with purchase schedules that meet the conditions stipulated in the supplier agreement. When a supplier has a problem meeting the schedule, it notifies the supplier scheduler, who in turn helps develop an alternative plan.

The supplier agreement approach, in my opinion, is an excellent first step for a retailer to take toward the eventual creation of product flow teams. Buyers are teamed up with distribution people; buyers plan and negotiate orders; and distribution people execute them. Later on, when appropriate, a store operations person joins the team. The addition of a store person should coincide with the implementation of DRP at the store level. In addition, if the retailer has already embraced the category manager concept, then it would make a great deal of sense to make the category manager the team leader and change his or her title to "product flow team manager." The current scope of a category manager, although an improvement in the buying world, is too narrow in scope for ECR. The advantage of a product flow team is that it can look at *all* the opportunities for saving money, from the time product is purchased to the time it is sold to the consumer; this is far beyond the scope of the category manager.

An ideal product flow team manager would have practical, hands-on experience in store operations, distribution, and buying. He or she would report to a director, who in turn reports to the top management team (see Figure 8-2 on p. 143). In this setting, customer product flow teams would interact with supplier product flow teams. Then, when conflicts arise or opportunities develop, recommendations can pass through up the organization, across companies, and back down to the product flow teams. This constitutes a "closed-loop management system" that can be extremely effective without turning the organizational chart upside down.

FIGURE 8-2: Closed-Loop Management Process

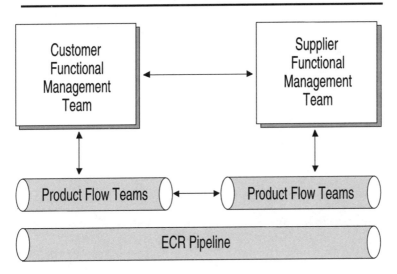

The product flow team concept provides a new basis for compensation, based on shared goals in three areas:

Area 1 (about 70 %) should be based on how well the team as a whole achieves its own objectives.

Area 2 (about 20 %) should be based on overall company profit performance.

Area 3 (about 10 %) should be based on shared objectives with a certain number of key suppliers' product flow teams. The third part should change from year to year and from supplier to supplier.

TRUST AND COOPERATION

ECR pipelines are based on a network of independent companies, suppliers, and customers, all linked by information technologies designed to remove cost and accelerate velocity. The network is linked by more than technology, however; trust is the "glue" that binds the partners together. Unfortunately, trust is often sorely lacking from business relationships today.

Consider how promotions are typically planned: they're almost always shrouded in mistrust and secrecy. While it makes sense for retailers not to broadcast their price planning and promotional dates to competitors, it's silly to be secretive with suppliers. Suppliers have nothing to gain and everything to lose by passing along one retailer's promotional plans to another. This would simply result in an internecine price war, scorched relationships, and further evidence that suppliers are not to be trusted. (The relationship between many retailers and manufacturing suppliers is already tense. Many of the comments I've heard are not fit to print. Suffice it to say that a good number of retailers are convinced that manufacturers are like boa constrictors, always squeezing them, and making too much money. Manufacturers, on the other hand, think that retailers are cheapskates who never want to pay for anything and always demand more.)

If an ECR pipeline is to become a reality, partners across the pipeline will have to work hard at creating trust and harmony.

DRP: THE "COOPERATION ENFORCER"

Nothing demands more cooperation than DRP, because it unifies all pipeline operations. Take a look at the typical DRP display shown in Figure 8-3. This display combines key information and creates an action plan. It starts with a sales forecast, considers inventory on order, takes in the inventory on-hand quantity, then calculates required future

FIGURE 8-3: Typical DRP Display

	Past Due	Day or Week							
		1	2	3	4	5	6	7	8
Sales Forecast		100	120	90	110	120	100	80	120
Inventory On Order									
Inventory On-Hand & Projected	500	400	280	490	380	260	460	380	260
Required Purchases		300			300				
Expected Receipts				300			300		

purchases and shows when they are expected to be received. Finally, DRP shows how much future inventory will exist (both on hand and projected).

If the sales forecast and expected receipts materialize as shown, the DRP display becomes the game plan that every product flow team across the distribution pipeline must execute. When you analyze the functions responsible for each line of information in the DRP display, and by type of company (retail, manufacturing, etc.), you'll end up with a set of core functions that must drive the product flow teams.

Figure 8-4 shows who, in retail, wholesale, and manufacturing, is (or should be) responsible for the various core functions (refer also to Figure 8-2).

Consider the sales forecast of the DRP display. In a retail setting, whoever is responsible for store operations is responsible for the forecast. In wholesale/distribution and manufacturing companies, the person responsible for the sales function is responsible for hitting the sales forecast.

Or, consider the required purchases line of the display. In retail and wholesale distribution companies, required

FIGURE 8-4: DRP Game Plan and Product Flow Teams

	Retailer	Wholesaler/Distributor	Manufacturer
Sales Forecast	Store Operations	Sales	Sales
Inventory On Order	Buyers	Buyers	Distribution
Inventory On-Hand & Projected	Distribution	Distribution	Distribution
Required Purchases	Buyers	Buyers	Distribution
Expected Receipts	Distribution	Distribution	Manufacturing

purchases are the domain of the buying organization. In manufacturing companies, required purchases are handled by the distribution/logistics organization.

As you can see, DRP can be used in a management process that unifies product flow teams within and across company boundaries. DRP provides people with the tools necessary for creating a pipeline-wide communications highway from store shelves to production lines. In addition, it formalizes communications through a common game plan. Individual company game plans are set and agreed to, then communicated to suppliers and integrated into their own game plan. Finally, DRP puts your most important asset—your people—in the driver's seat.

My mentor, MRP pioneer Oliver Wight, used to say, "Give me the best system in the world, and if my people don't know how to use it, I'll fail. Give me well-educated and well-trained people, and a system that limps along, and I'll get by. But give me well-educated and well-trained people and the best system in the world, and stand back!"

CHAPTER 9

Implementing ECR: A Blueprint for Success

Although the systems needed to make ECR a reality are relatively new to the retail world, they've been well tested and proven in other distribution environments. Take Distribution Resource Planning, (DRP), which is far and away the most important, far-reaching system re quired of all infopartners that agree to participate in ECR pipelines. Over the last eighteen years, manufacturers and wholesaler/distributors have been successfully implementing DRP in their distribution operations. Many times, companies don't take advantage of this experience. Instead, they do what comes naturally, which unfortunately points them in the wrong direction—toward software and hardware rather than in the direction of people and business programs, data accuracy, and accountability. Fortunately, there is a set of directions; in this chapter, I'll discuss those directions in the context of implementing DRP.

THE ROAD THAT SHOULD BE TAKEN

The implementation plan for DRP is based on the accumulated experience of hundreds of companies over nearly twenty years. The good news about the implementation plan is that it's not just theoretical speculation by armchair experts. The bad news is that it requires some work. But even though the implementation plan requires a concerted effort, it requires far less energy than doing two implementations: an "initial flop" and a subsequent "redo." In addition to the out-of-pocket costs, companies often incur far more serious hidden costs in terms of frustrating and demoralizing their workforces by going a second round.

Another incentive for using the implementation plan to get rolling is to sit down and calculate the cost in terms of *not* doing the implementation for one month. This is done by taking the annual projected savings from DRP, subtracting the annual operating costs, then dividing the result by 12. In a typical organization, the annual savings typically work out at several million dollars per year. Let's say a company takes an implementation shortcut such as not investing in data accuracy, or makes a poor choice, like failing to do some basic work in forecasting. Or, let's say it skips the education phase. Any one of these could easily derail the implementation by three or four months, costing the company at least $1 million and probably more. So, on a strictly financial basis, the implementation plan is well worth the effort.

RETAILERS, WHOLESALERS, AND MANUFACTURERS IMPLEMENTING A CUSTOMER-DRIVEN CPR

Figure 9-1 shows a graphic representation of the implementation plan. You might want to refer to the illustration as I describe the twelve major steps below.

FIGURE 9-1: Implementation Plan—Retailer/Wholesaler

Education / Consulting			
Audit	Demand Management	Pilot	
Project Organization	Supplier Scheduling	Performance Measures	Audit
Performance Goals	Data Integrity		
	Software		
Coordination with Manufacturers			

Step 1. Initial Audit

This step is a means of assessing where a company is today, in order to establish a starting point for the implementation. It identifies the greatest opportunities and the most urgent priorities. Often, an audit is done by working with an outside consultant using an accepted checklist.

- a short-term action plan—what do you do next;
- identification of opportunities.

Step 2. Education/Consulting

The goal of the education/consulting phase is to give the key management group an understanding of what is involved in the implementation process. It is fairly typical in many organizations for significant misunderstandings and differing expectations to exist both within the management team and among the employees.

Some people may see DRP as a computer system—"put two programmers on it for three months and you're there." Others may see it as a purchasing system, in which case, why would you need any involvement from other areas such as distribution? Other people again see it as a companywide system, integrating the different groups into a team effort that unifies all departments with a single set of numbers. And still other people think they're so unique and different that DRP won't work for them. All but one of these is a misunderstanding. If the management team is composed of people who have these different opinions, then there's little likelihood that they'll send a consistent message to the rest of the company.

When the management team cannot communicate a consistent message, people use a lot of their time trying to figure out what DRP is, and what their managers want them to do, *rather than implementing it*. In most organizations, a tremendous amount of energy that could be used on implementation tasks is wasted trying to understand what is *expected*. Therefore, it's critical for a management group to send consistent messages.

The payoff from clear and consistent messages from top management can be significant. Many companies only apply a small percentage of their available "horsepower" to the implementation tasks, because their people either lack clear direction or they sense a lack of commitment. By eliminating inconsistent messages, a management team can almost double the available horsepower. Best of all, it doesn't cost a cent to communicate a consistent message, nor does it take a tremendous amount of time.

The education/consulting phase is where a management team learns what ECR is all about, and how it can apply the approach to its own company. It's important for the key management group to reach a consensus about the benefits of the implementation, as well as the necessary resources. Most companies have their top management team (the president and the president's staff) attend a seminar. They also have the key middle managers who will be involved in the implementation process (representatives from purchasing, distribution, finance, store operations, and Management Information Systems (MIS)) attend a similar but more detailed seminar. Each of these people will play an important role in defining the benefits and understanding their department's involvement; consequently, each needs a working understanding of the technologies being implemented.

After the seminar, the top management group meets and works to reach a consensus on the benefits to the company and the resources that will be required. This consensus helps give a consistent message to the rest of the organization. The top managers can work out differences among themselves, rather than have their people bump into one another in the hall, compare notes, and create confusion.

Following this initial phase of education, there is a more detailed education and consulting phase, designed to educate the mass of people in a company, the people who will make the new ways of doing business work.

Sadly, most companies do as little education as they think

they can get away with, and the education they do is usually modeled on basic childhood schooling. In this model, a teacher has the information and communicates it to the "students," who soak it all up, then go back and do their work differently. The flow is one way—from teacher to student. And the outcome is predetermined. For example, discussing the Revolutionary War isn't going to change who won, just as discussing origins of algebra isn't going to change the rules of mathematics.

The point is, although this model may work well for the fourth grade, it's not effective for introducing change in an organization. It generates low levels of enthusiasm and ownership—both of which are necessary for change to actually happen. A better model is the business meeting. In a business meeting, the leader may know more than others in the room, but nobody has all the answers—the meeting runs on the collective knowledge of the participants. Because this approach recognizes the experience and intelligence of the people in the organization, it builds high levels of ownership and enthusiasm, and it produces better decisions.

Step 3. Project Organization

Although some of the terms are different from company to company, Figure 9-2 illustrates the groups and people generally involved in an implementation.

The *project team* is responsible for the day-to-day management of the implementation. Project team members represent their different functional areas. For example, the team would have representatives (typically the department heads) from purchasing, distribution, MIS, store operations, finance, and so on. The members of the project team manage implementation tasks, and may also do closer work

FIGURE 9-2: Project Organization

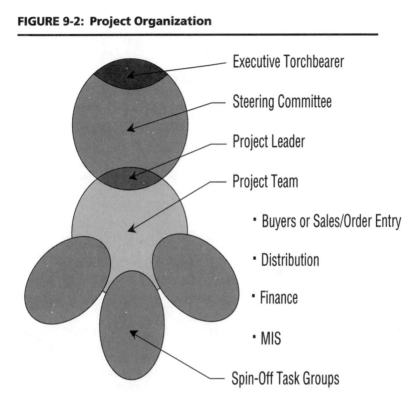

- Executive Torchbearer
- Steering Committee
- Project Leader
- Project Team
  - Buyers or Sales/Order Entry
  - Distribution
  - Finance
  - MIS
- Spin-Off Task Groups

on these tasks. A project team member may, for instance, undertake responsibility for working with the store operations to develop procedures to assure 95 percent inventory record accuracy. The project team typically meets weekly.

The executive *steering committee* members are concerned less with tactics and more with strategy and resources—they focus on the overall management of the project and make major decisions, such as, "Do we have the resources needed to produce forecasts?" or, "Are we going to implement DRP at the stores as well as the distribution centers?"

If there's a management problem, the project team needs

to raise the flag and alert the steering committee. The steering committee in turn needs to make whatever decisions or get whatever resources are needed to correct the situation. For example, the project may be in trouble because the accuracy of the inventory records is lagging and creating difficulties. The steering company would then need to ask, "Do we delay the implementation until the accuracy is up to 95 percent, or do we implement at the distribution centers, and delay the store-level implementation for six months?" *Overall responsibility for the success of the implementation rests with the steering committee.*

The project team leader is also a member of the executive steering committee, and serves as the primary interface between the two groups. He or she attends all the steering committee meetings, and updates the steering committee on the progress of the implementation tasks.

The *executive torchbearer* represents the top management group, and takes personal responsibility for the success of the implementation. The torchbearer is the person with the "fire in the belly" needed to make the implementation happen. The executive torchbearer puts his or her reputation on the line. In addition, one of the torchbearer's most important roles is to defend the implementation against diversions. Most companies have more good ideas and more good initiatives than they have the resources to implement. Consequently, someone needs to keep the organization focused on bringing the current implementations through to completion.

Spinoff task groups are small groups assigned to various tasks. These tasks could include revising the process for how a buyer does his or her job; developing more of a flow through the distribution center; working to create models for forecasting; and so on. The spinoff task groups are important for several reasons. First, they are a practical way to get work done in an organization that is overloaded already. Rather than having the burden of work fall on a small group, like the project team, it's spread among a larger number of people. In addition, better decisions are made when the people closest to a situation are part of the problem-solving process.

Finally, spreading the work also spreads the ownership. One of the primary objectives of the implementation is to have people take "ownership" in both the changes and the new ways of running the business. By including significant numbers of people in the implementation process, these people have had a say in the changes, and feel they have "ownership" in the new processes.

The spinoff task forces need to be coordinated so that the different groups aren't doing things in conflict with each other, or wasting significant time and energy by duplicating activities. There are several ways to handle coordination. One is to put the burden of coordination on the spinoff teams, making them responsible for checking with the other teams to make sure their activities are complimentary. Another approach is to have one member of the project team on each spinoff task group, so that the groups are coordinated through the project team.

Step 4. Performance Goals

While the initial audit (step 1) identifies where you are today, performance goals represent the *quantitative* measure of what you expect to achieve in the future. It's important to describe these goals in advance, so everyone knows clearly what's expected of him or her.

Performance goals should be stated concretely, as in, "We expect an improvement in customer service from 95 to 99 percent." . . . "We expect a 20 percent reduction in inventory." [and] "a 5 percent reduction in purchase and administrative costs."

If the performance goals are not set properly, you run the risk of everyone developing a different set of expectations about what "acceptable" performance means. You might hear questions like, "Well, we lowered inventory by 3 percent—that's certainly good, isn't it?" Or, "We increased productivity in purchasing by 4 percent—that's better than the national average, isn't it?" The best performance goals are "stretch" goals that challenge and motivate people.

Finally, performance goals must be meaningful in terms of the competitive equation. After all, if a company goes to all the time and expense of implementing new ways to run the business and only sets goals of 2 or 3 percent improvement, this communicates a low self-assessment in terms of what the management and the workforce are capable of doing. In fact, a talented and aggressive management team should be able to realize substantial improvements.

Step 5. Demand Management

Many retailers do little in the way of forecasting. It's typical for most companies to use a four-week moving average in their purchasing systems to suggest orders to the buyers. To be effective in providing good projections for purchasing, distribution, and suppliers, it's necessary to invest some effort in attempting to predict the future demand streams for each product.

History is the best starting point for this task. Many companies have several years of history for their products, including the timing and nature of promotions. That information can be used to develop baseline forecasts by having the computer remove the promotional spikes. The spikes can then be used to anticipate the effect of a particular type of promotion, the result being an historical forecast that indicates the baseline demand and promotional "lift." The buyer or demand manager can then add any promotional increases where promotions are scheduled and based on prior promotional experience. If this data is not available, you can purchase databases that contain the same type of information.

Step 6. Supplier Scheduling

This step involves communication of the supplier schedules. Typically, these schedules are communicated as electronic transactions (using the UCS 830 format). Some retailers/wholesalers are equipped to send these transactions and some manufacturers are equipped to receive them; in other cases, this work must be done by acquiring the necessary systems and technology.

In addition to the mechanics of the supplier schedule, several business issues must be resolved. For example, will the retailer review the planned orders in DRP and convert them to purchase orders? Ideally, the answer would be no. Rather, the retailer would transmit the schedule, and the manufacturer would convert the information into shipments based on its internal lead times so that the products arrive by the dates the retailers have specified. Such agreements must be made part of this implementation step.

Step 7. Data Integrity

In his book *MRP II: Making It Happen* (Oliver Wight, 1985), Tom Wallace explains that there are two types of data: "forgiving" and "unforgiving." Let's take a look at both types and how they effect the planning and scheduling systems used to drive ECR.

"Unforgiving" Data. Unforgiving data is the type that causes serious problems if it's not accurate. In a DRP environment, such data includes inventory record accuracy at the distribution centers, stores, and distribution networks.

If the inventory records are incorrect, the planning will be wrong. If you think you have one hundred cases of light bulbs in the DC and you only have fifty, then the planned orders will be incorrect, creating incorrect distribution plans, incorrect supplier schedules, and so on. Similarly, if you think you have five cases in the store, and you really have just one, then you will most likely have an out-of-stock situation in the stores, as well as incorrect distribution information, incorrect demands on the distribution center, and incorrect supplier schedules.

It's also important to represent the distribution network accurately. If a particular store is supplied by a particular distribution center, then it's important to show this correctly within the system. Otherwise, the demands from that store will not show up as demand at the right distribution center, and this will create possible out-of-stock situations, incorrect demands on the distribution center, and incorrect supplier schedules.

The necessary data accuracy levels for effective operation are: inventory records—95 percent; and distribution networks—98 percent. Note that the 95 percent inventory record accuracy is not calculated in net dollars (the way accounting measures a physical inventory). Using the net dollars method, an error of $+50$ cases on clear light bulbs, and an error of -50 cases on frosted light bulbs, results in a very small error, or no error, in terms of dollars. Such an error has little impact on the company's financial books, yet it can have a *significant* impact on the company's ability to satisfy customers because the DRP schedules for both products will be wrong.

The target of 95 percent inventory record accuracy used for DRP means that 95 percent of the SKUs are within the counting tolerance for that item. If one hundred items were cycle-counted, and ten were found to have differences between the on-hand balance and the actual count that were greater than the counting tolerance, the resulting accuracy would be 90 percent. The tolerance is generally based on how the items are counted: zero percent for case packaged items; 2 percent or so for weigh counted items, like apples.

The levels of accuracy for most retailers and wholesalers at the distribution centers already exceed 95 percent. The implementation challenge lies in achieving this level of accuracy at the store level. Accuracy of scanned data becomes an issue in this context, because of the use of the multiplier key; as we've discussed earlier, while scanning one flavor of cat food instead of capturing each can will get customers through the checkout line quickly, it will compromise the accuracy of the on-hand balance even faster.

A distribution network accuracy of 98 percent means that 98 percent of the networks show the correct store to DC connection, and DC to supplier connection. If three network connections are tested, and one shows an incorrect store to DC connection, the resulting accuracy is 66 percent.

You may wonder, "Do we really have the ability to achieve such high levels of accuracy?" The answer is a resounding yes! There is a tested and proven process for achieving inventory record accuracy, and distribution network accuracy.

It's done every day, by companies populated by mortal human beings. That process includes the following steps:

1. Educate people so that they understand why it's important to have accurate information, and how other companies have been successful in achieving the established goals.
2. Assign responsibility to an individual or a group for the accuracy of the records.
3. Provide the tools: you need a simple and easy-to-use transaction recording system.
4. Audit the accuracy. For inventory records, the most common method is cycle counting, where a sample of items are counted on a periodic basis and compared to the on-hand balance.
5. Correct the causes of errors. The primary purpose of the audits is to find and fix the causes of the inaccurate data. In the same way that you cannot "inspect quality into a product," you cannot "audit accuracy into the information." It is not possible to cycle-count your way to 95 percent inventory record accuracy—the root causes of the errors must be uncovered, and corrected.

"Forgiving" Data. With forgiving data, "reasonable" accuracy is acceptable—and generally fairly easy to get. The forgiving data include order quantities, lead times, and safety stock levels. Of course, there are several "right" numbers for each of these. If the order quantity is two days of supply, is three days of supply incorrect? No, two days may be better than three days, but neither is "wrong." The objective is to get to the point where you are ordering a little of each item every day (what you think you'll need tomorrow), not determining a "right" order quantity.

Safety stock is a function of the uncertainty in either demand or supply. If demand is fairly unpredictable, then more safety stock will be needed. If supply is uncertain due to transportation problems, for example, then more safety stock is needed. Again, the objective is to do a better job of predicting the demand and managing distribution so safety stocks can be safely reduced.

With respect to lead times, the objective is to provide a supplier schedule so that lead time becomes a meaningless concept. The suppliers will be seeing the schedules several weeks into the future, and will convert planned demands into actual shipments in time to meet the delivery requirements. In this infopartnering environment, there is a need for buyers to maintain only reasonable lead times for all the different SKUs.

Step 8. Software

Although software is essential for DRP, the best software package is no guarantee of top-notch performance. What correlates with excellent performance is good management. To make an analogy with golf, it's not the cost of the set of clubs, but how you hit the ball.

Today, there is good, tested DRP software. Over the years, a number of companies have attempted to write their own software. While there are one or two successes, the overwhelming majority of these experiences have been disasters. The typical DRP software package represents an investment of more than fifty man-years of systems and programming work. Even if a company were to put five or ten people on the project (which is the most that can be used efficiently), the effort would still extend beyond the total time frame for implementation.

The best analogy for DRP software is that of the catapult

on an aircraft carrier. The catapult takes the airplane from zero to 170 miles per hour in a little over three seconds. But after that, the airplane's own engines have to do the work. Similarly, a software package gets a company from zero to 100 man-years of systems effort in a few months, but then it's the company's responsibility to adapt the package to its specific needs and maintain the software. Every company does have individual needs, but these typically require only minor changes in the software to make the package work. Typical customization jobs might be the reformatting of a picking list or the addition of a particular calculation to determine the quantity that should initially be distributed to the stores on a promotion.

Step 9. Coordination with Manufacturers

By working together, retailers or wholesalers and manufacturers have the opportunity to significantly reduce costs throughout the distribution pipeline. It's essential that DRP be put into place to establish the framework for this reduction. For this reason, there are a number of technical issues to be resolved between the retailers or wholesalers and manufacturers. These include the content of the 830 transaction that carries the data on planned shipments to the manufacturer. They also include agreement on who does the load building. Is the retailer going to do the load building and send planned orders that have already been sized into truckload quantities to the manufacturers, or are the retailers or wholesalers going to transmit their demands and have the manufacturer build the load?

Bear in mind that the technical system only opens the door to larger improvements—it doesn't force them to happen. For example, in many businesses there are significant opportunities for cost reduction in the distribution pipeline, but these require changes in the business relationships between the companies.

Manufacturers often work overtime in anticipation of a deal period, and rent warehouse space to store the necessary inventory. Retailers often buy more than they need during the promotion period because of the price incentives. Consequently, they may also have to rent storage space and do extra handling to hold this inventory. Also, the consumer gets products that are less fresh than those that have been kept moving in the distribution pipeline. In other words, this is a classic "lose-lose" situation.

Why not encourage retailers to commit to sizable quantities, but take delivery in synch with the way the marketplace consumes it (cf. the section on forward commit in Chapter 4)? This is the type of change in basic business practices that should be examined at this phase of the implementation. Other areas include reducing administration and paperwork. Manufacturing companies have dramatically streamlined the overhead in the customer-supplier relationship using "Just-in-Time" approaches. The same types of opportunities are available in the retailer/manufacturer relationship.

Step 10. Pilot

There are three ways to begin using a new system like DRP:

1. *Parallel approach.* This is great if you're replacing a system that already does what the new system does. Take payroll—you can simultaneously run the old and the new payroll systems and compare the checks as they come out of both systems. If the checks match over a period of time, you can safely disconnect the old system and run on the new

one. The problem is that most companies are implementing a DRP system for the first time, not replacing one piece of software with another, so they don't have a system that gives them the same information that they can compare against the new system.

2. *"Cold turkey."* This is appealing to many people, but it's not recommended. "Cold turkey" means you throw the switch on Friday, and you're on the new system by Monday—all items, all products, everything at once. Some people argue that this approach forces everyone to sink or swim on Monday. But, in fact, it might sink the entire operation. As Oliver Wight CEO Walt Goddard puts it, "The drowning man doesn't die from lack of motivation; he's overwhelmed." If your data isn't as accurate as it should be, and if your people aren't as well trained as they need to be, then you run the risk of major chaos, reduced shipments, and financial pain. A few companies have survived a cold turkey cutover, but most suffer major damage. Not surprisingly, those that have survived a cold turkey cutover swear they'd never do it again.

3. *Pilot approach.* This is the recommended approach. The pilot is a "cold turkey," but applied only to a limited number of items—you "flip the switch" on a small enough piece of the business so there is low risk if things go wrong. No one will be overwhelmed. You can fix whatever problems appear, and continue doing business. After about a month of pilot, you'll have identified most of the problems. Once you've fixed them, it's time to take another group of products and begin running them on the new system. Fix the problems that emerge, settle in, and continue, until all products have been included. Clearly, this is the least risky and most orderly approach, the one most likely to lead to a

successful implementation, and the one pursued by nearly all companies these days.

There are really three pilots. The first is the "software" pilot, which is used to test the software and make sure it's working as expected. The second is the "conference room" pilot. This is an extension of the education/consulting phase, where you work with the system using your data, and simulate how you would use the system. The third is the "live" pilot, and entails using the system to plan and schedule the pilot items.

Step 11. Performance Measurements

How do you know that the pilot is working? How do you know whether to continue with it or to fix it? Some of these questions can be answered subjectively. "Do people believe the schedules?" "Are you getting good information?" Yet there are other questions that can only be answered by establishing performance measurements.

Some of the measurements or goals that you set for yourself won't be apparent in the pilot program—it's unlikely that overall customer service will improve significantly with just a pilot program. So you might start tracking customer service on specific product lines. Some companies compare items that are on the pilot and items that are not. The same holds with productivity, although that's more difficult to measure on a product-by-product basis.

The key issue at this point is to start measuring against the goals. One thing that people often don't realize is that the planning and scheduling system just clears the water—making previously hidden problems visible. The problems don't go away just because you can see them. But at least people can see what has to be done.

Step 12. Second Audit

"Where are we?" "Did we achieve the goals we set for ourselves in the beginning?" "What's next?" "What other things should we be working on?"

The initial audit identified the opportunities for improvement, and triggered a series of implementation activities. If those activities worked well, then the operation of the business has improved significantly. The second audit might reveal that, while you've done certain things well—such as data accuracy—you are not managing DRP well. Perhaps the forecasting process is not up to snuff. These kinds of deficiencies would become apparent through the second audit. You can then focus on the problems, and pour your energy into fixing them.

It also may be the case that you've done all of the steps quite well—not 100 percent, but approaching excellence—and now you need to consider implementing other technologies that were not included in your first effort. The world doesn't stand still; what was competitive two years ago may not be so today. The second audit can point you in the right direction.

IMPLEMENTATION PLAN FOR A MANUFACTURER WORKING WITH A RETAILER OR A WHOLESALER

Figure 9-3 shows a graphic representation of the implementation steps for a manufacturer working in partnership with a retailer or wholesaler. Many of the steps are the same, such as the education/consulting used to train people on the new system, and the establishment of performance goals against which the company will measure itself

FIGURE 9-3: Implementation Plan for a Manufacturer

Education / Consulting			
Project Organization	Demand Management	Pilot	
Performance Goals	Software	Performance Measures	Audit
Coordination with Retailers			

after the implementation. Below, I've identified the few areas of difference.

Project Organization (STEP #3)

Typically, the sales organization from the manufacturer is a part of the implementation team shown in Figure 9-2, replacing the purchasing organization. This provides an implementation team for the manufacturer that is almost a mirror image of the team for the retailer/wholesaler.

Demand Management (STEP #5)

A manufacturer may have to deal with a number of different demand streams, as explained earlier. For example, a manufacturer may have some customers that are using DRP and supplying them with planned orders (UCS 830s). Another group of customers may be doing supplier-driven continuous replenishment, and expects the manufacturer to identify when to ship product to either their stores or distribution centers. In these cases, it is the responsibility of the manufacturer to forecast and plan the SKUs for these customers. Finally, there are the customers doing business the old way. They send purchase orders but otherwise provide little or no visibility beyond the current week or two.

Most manufacturers don't have the systems to integrate these three different demand streams into a single accurate stream that is then fed into a master scheduling system. The work involved in this step is to either modify the current forecasting and master scheduling systems to forecast only the customers doing business the old way, then show the demand stream from the continuous replenishment customers as a forecast to the master scheduling system, take the planned orders from their DRP customers, and feed them directly into its master scheduling system as a forecast of shipments. This work does need to be done, especially as more and more companies depart from the traditional way of doing business.

Data Integrity (STEP # 7)

"Data integrity" in this context applies to the integrity in the manufacturer's facilities. With all the effort going into the development of accurate demand streams, an incorrect inventory balance at the manufacturer's distribution center or plant could reduce or eliminate the cost savings that would occur in the distribution channel.

RESOURCE CONFLICTS

One of the basic principles of implementation is ownership. A guaranteed route to frustration and failure is to have someone go into a dark room, redesign someone else's job, and present it to them as carved in stone. By spreading the load to as many people in the organization as possible, you'll accomplish two important goals. First, you'll reduce the demands that fall on any one person. Second, because many different people are actively involved in the work and decision-making process, "ownership" of the changes is much higher than would otherwise be the case.

A major issue in implementation is how much you can realistically do within a given time frame. It's better to say you're going to do less and make it happen than to make big promises and then not deliver. If the task is manageable and people achieve success, everyone will be motivated to take on additional challenges. If people can never be winners, they'll be demotivated and the entire organization will achieve less. An excellent test of the maturity of a management team is its ability to set realistic goals and objectives for its people. You may need everything yesterday, but if it can't be done, your management team needs to step up to their responsibilities and produce realistic plans.

The methodology of implementation described in this chapter is a proven approach that has withstood the test of time very successfully in retail, wholesale/distribution, and manufacturing companies. If you follow the implementation plan, you will have erased the potential for dealing with an enormous challenge—reimplementation after an initial failure. As you will see in the next chapter, seven key challenges must be met, by all means avoid adding more!

CHAPTER 10

The Road Ahead: Opportunities and Challenges in the Era of Infopartnering and ECR

It's a safe bet that infopartnering, based on resource planning and scheduling systems and other currently available tools, will become the overwhelmingly dominant methodology in the field of retail and wholesale logistics in the next ten years. As I hope I've shown throughout this book, it is vastly superior to conventional methods of managing the flow of product across a distribution pipeline. It has a proven track record in retail, wholesale, and manufacturing. It has the flexibility to deal with high/low, as well as EDLP (everyday low-price) operators. And it is the only management process that has the capability to schedule an entire distribution pipeline, connect it in a seamless manner, and reduce operating costs so that all partners enjoy savings that can be passed on to the final consumer.

MAJOR OPPORTUNITIES

The moment that a consumer product moves off the production line today, it spends 90 percent of its time sitting in inventory until it is finally purchased by the consumer in a retail store. Based on my experience, it is very possible with infopartnering to move inventory 50 percent of the time (some mass merchandisers are already doing so in certain product categories). This reduction translates into a five-fold improvement in inventory turns across a given distribution pipeline.

The goal for all distribution pipelines must be increased inventory velocity, combined with the removal of any unnecessary activities. The longer companies wait to shift into "high-velocity gear," the longer they'll miss the opportunity to save tens of millions of dollars per year. Further, competition that adopts a high-velocity approach will soon steal market share, because of the significant cost advantage it will be able to achieve.

Not everyone, of course, will be a survivor. History shows that when there are high rates of change, the cards get shuffled; that is, there will be a new pecking order. Companies on the cutting edge today may be on the bleeding edge tomorrow. Those companies that wait may well find themselves surpassed by competitors that have adopted and become proficient in DRP, and have been transformed into effective infopartners.

For companies that adopt the ECR vision and enter into infopartnerships, much will change. Things will no longer be measured in terms of weeks and months, but rather in terms of *hours* and *days*. Take inventory as an example. It will not be uncommon to find distribution pipelines operating with 20 to 30 days of supply, as opposed to 80 to 120 days, as is typical today. Imagine the positive impact this has on a company's profit and loss and balance sheet. Net retail operating margins will more than double or triple, and the huge amounts of working capital freed up in inventories will be used to grow, expand, and modernize. Pipeline partners will use information instead of inventory, while others continue to build warehouses at $50 million a shot for the purpose of sitting on inventory instead of selling it.

In addition to lower overhead, infopartners will have lower labor costs and fresher products. Their systems will perform most of the routine tasks, so that people can be freed up to do more creative and innovative work. They will also have the luxury of more productive store shelf space, and the capability of offering greater product variety despite the reduction in overall inventory.

Before they can achieve this enviable position and enjoy the opportunities for greater profitability, though, they'll need to meet a number of tough challenges—which I'll describe in the remainder of this chapter.

THE SEVEN CHALLENGES OF INFOPARTNERING AHEAD

Many challenges lie ahead on the road to successful infopartnering. Seven are particularly critical and merit discussion:

1. Adopting a willingness to change existing business practices.
2. Elevating logistics to a high-level executive concern.
3. Investing in knowledge acquisition.
4. Adopting the product flow team concept.

5. Mastering the distribution component of the marketing mix.
6. Measuring the right things.
7. Transforming leaders into coaches.

ADOPTING A WILLINGNESS TO CHANGE EXISTING BUSINESS PRACTICES

Today, companies involved in distribution pipelines need to think seriously about lopping off practices that ultimately lead to diminished profits and inefficiencies, such as slotting allowances, nonperforming co-op ads, failure fees, forward buying, diverting, free cases, and bill backs. Dropping or changing such practices won't be easy—they're deeply ingrained in the way we do business, and many have become "standard operating practice" over the years, with too few questioning why they're done.

For example, as most business professionals know all too well, companies play games every month, quarter, or year-end to make the sales numbers come out "right." Changing these business practices and selling what consumers need and want will cause a painful, but necessary, one-time sales adjustment. Top management must have the courage to stand up and explain to its shareholders that profits were down temporarily because the company decided to stop selling consumers products they don't need.

To succeed in the age of infopartnering, *every* business practice must be placed under the microscope and then subjected to the "value test." (By "value," I mean better product quality, freshness, assortment, lower prices, and better service.) Any practice that fails to add value should be slated for demolition.

Practices deemed unacceptable for business in the info-partnering age must be replaced by alternatives that benefit everyone in the distribution pipeline. Manufacturers can be of tremendous help here by making it possible for retail and wholesaler/distributor partners to adopt win-win practices without having to pay a financial penalty. A prime example is forward commit (see Chapter 4), which offers all the advantages of forward buys, but doesn't require anyone to carry an onerous inventory burden. In addition, it smooths out manufacturing peaks and inventory buildups across the distribution pipeline, so that everyone benefits from higher inventory velocity.

Simplify, Simplify, Simplify!

The old acronym in computer programming, "KISS"—"Keep it simple, stupid"—has significant import for business today. Simplification is a great way to clean house and vanquish inappropriate business practices. This is especially true of practices related to overhead. Many companies that use distribution and manufacturing resource planning and scheduling systems, for example, have been able to completely eliminate purchase orders with key suppliers. In return, these same suppliers no longer issue invoices to those customers. Both the customer and the supplier use a new business practice, which entails working to a supplier schedule communicated electronically via EDI. These schedules are equivalent to purchase contracts, with scheduled delivery dates and quantities. They carry purchase order numbers, but no purchase order document per se is ever issued. The PO numbers are used for cross-reference to identify what is received against a schedule. Suppliers send monthly statements in lieu of individual invoices with every shipment.

Just think about the tremendous advantage such an approach offers in overhead reduction and product receiving activities, as well as in accounts payables on the customer side. For the supplier, think of the savings in order entry, billing, and accounts receivables departments. Eliminating purchase orders is but one of many examples where existing business practices can be simplified, saving a significant amount of money in unnecessary overhead costs. Just by questioning the status quo, companies will find a wealth of opportunities for saving money, time, and energy—all valuable commodities in the age of infopartnering.

ELEVATING LOGISTICS TO A HIGH-LEVEL EXECUTIVE CONCERN

For too long, the world of distribution and logistics—and, to a certain extent, the world of manufacturing—has been viewed as the domain of cigar chompers, beefy-armed truckers, and "metal benders." It smacks of the boredom of doing a repetitive job five or six days a week, and conjures up the smell of sweat, diesel fuel, and corrugated boxes, as well as the constant grating din of pallet jacks and forklifts. As a consequence, senior management often doesn't know, nor does it appreciate, what goes on in the logistics and manufacturing side of its own business. As a rule, CEOs and other senior officers hail from the sales or financial side of the company, and have little connection with the logistics or manufacturing "wings." The same holds true for other executives who participate in top management decisions—most have never visited a distribution center or factory, let alone picked an order or loaded a truck.

A high-level executive once told me, "I visited our people in the distribution center the other day to shake hands and congratulate them on the signature of our new three-year labor contract. The folks were in great spirits, and the place was spotless." When I left this person's office, another manager who had been present told me that the whole thing was a "ritual": this key executive only visited the logistics people when it was time to sign a labor contract. Sure, they were in "great spirits"!

The key executive in question was completely out of touch with the logistics people, and didn't have the foggiest notion about what makes his distribution pipeline hum. Like some top executives, I suspect that he considered the distribution/logistics function as a necessary evil for getting stuff from A to B, and a functional area plagued with problems that generate nasty remarks from suppliers and even store operations.

The negative image of logistics is further perpetuated by the fact that it is traditionally assumed to be a cost center that drags down profits. Adding to the bad rap, logistics is plagued by accidents and workmen's compensation, making it an expensive nuisance.

Clearly, if companies are going to become infopartners and achieve the ECR vision, their top executives will have to dramatically change their attitude toward the distribution/logistics end of their businesses. I believe that the Kurt Salmon study is conservative when it states that 40 percent of the $30 billion potential savings (in the grocery sector alone) will be saved through so-called efficient replenishment. When the dust settles and we look back on how we achieved the lion's share of the savings, we will find that it came from distribution/logistics. That's because inventories across a given distribution pipeline are like giant magnets that attract most of the cost of doing business from the moment it leaves the production line to the time it is purchased off the retail store shelves by the consumer.

Guess who's in the best position to bring down inventory-related costs? It's your local logistics/distribution professionals. As top executives need to learn, such people are not gnomes who tiptoe around a subterranean world in which products are boxed and moved through an underground network. No, these people have worked in the dark for too long. It's high time they should bask in the limelight and enjoy the recognition that they sorely deserve!

INVESTING IN KNOWLEDGE ACQUISITION

At this moment, the greatest obstacle to achieving the ECR vision is a paucity of knowledge about how to effectively manage a distribution pipeline. How many seasoned executives or practitioners know:

- the difference between independent and dependent demand, or that the two types even exist?
- that uncertainty of demand in a given distribution pipeline only exists at the point of final sale?
- that we live in a scheduling world when we manufacture and distribute products from factories to retail store shelves?
- that a distribution pipeline is filled with constraints that inhibit the flow of product if the product needs and capacity needs are not in perfect equilibrium?

I could continue this line of questioning for many pages, but the extent of our current state of knowledge about infopartnering principles isn't the issue; the key point is that when it comes to managing the dynamics of a distribution pipeline, most companies are rookies. It's not enough to want to be an enthusiastic supporter—companies engaging in infopartnering must *know precisely* what they need to do and how to go about doing it. And that all starts with in-depth knowledge about the fundamental dynamics of pipeline management.

The onus is on top management, starting with the CEO, to acquire the basic knowledge about pipeline dynamics and how each infopartner in the pipeline can work both independently and as a member of a team to accelerate the flow of product and to reduce costs. The CEO must then make it possible for that knowledge to flow down through the rest of the organization to the people who will make infopartnering a day-to-day reality.

ADOPTING THE PRODUCT FLOW TEAM CONCEPT

Moving to product flow teams is going to be a major challenge for most companies. First, people who have been used to doing things a certain way will have to learn new ways. Second, the path will be filled with such perils as turf issues, functional empires, bloated egos, power-hungry people, fear and loathing, and other land mines that stand in the way of teamwork. Painful as it may be, each info-partner must adopt the flow team mentality, provide the right training to flow team members, and hand out well-focused game plans.

An effective approach to breaking down barriers such as turf issues is to ask all those who oppose the move to PFTs the basic question: What is best for the company? Rarely do people think of what is best for the company first; most came up through the ranks as functional experts and usually think in terms of what's best for their own department.

For product flow teams to exist and to succeed, everyone must shift into a "horizontal" mind-set that focuses on how product flows from point A to point B. To achieve that new focus, product flow teams must be educated and trained in the art of sales forecasting, demand and inventory management, procurement, and distribution execution (which includes warehouse and transportation management), rather than in what's important to know in order to manage their own departments.

To be effective, the product flow teams must have the knowledge, the right tools, and the information necessary to move product in the most efficient manner. After moving product from A to B (e.g., from a factory to a distribution center), the product flow team will then work with the customer flow teams so that goods can be shipped the most efficient way possible to the customer's location.

Top management can help immensely here, first by mandating a move to product flow teams; second, by ensuring that team members are given the chance to acquire the necessary knowledge to get the job done; third, by ensuring that reporting responsibilities are formalized and officially announced; and fourth, by deciding that compensation is based on shared objectives (see Chapter 8).

Top management's commitment is clearly necessary to make product flow teams happen. When top management does get behind the PFT concept, it sends a very powerful message that the company is taking ECR extremely seriously and is totally committed to its success.

MASTERING THE DISTRIBUTION COMPONENT OF THE MARKETING MIX

Infopartnering is designed to help infopartners provide the right products and services to specific customers at the lowest possible price. This means retail, wholesale, and manufacturing companies all must apply the concept of "micromarketing"—and apply it very well. If they don't, it's unlikely that individual retail stores will be able to develop merchandising strategies that offer customers the products and services they seek at the lowest possible cost.

To accomplish this objective, it's essential that the proper infosystems be implemented, right down to the store level of detail. Store demographics—such as rate of sale by product by store, and ethnic trend wants and needs—represent but one type of information necessary for micromarketing. There are many other opportunities in this area.

One major opportunity entails mastering the "sleeping giant" of the marketing mix: product, price, distribution, and promotion. I believe it is safe to say that the three "p's" of the marketing mix (product, price, promotion) are easy to clone across competitors. The fourth, distribution, is somewhat different. To a marketing professional, the term "distribution" usually means "distribution exclusivity" or "distribution margin." In other words, it is thought of in terms of channels defining distribution selected to sell products.

Finally, while these four elements of the mix are important to a marketing sales professional, to achieve true ECR, executives must focus heavily on the fifth element— the flip side of distribution that begs the question, "Is my product constantly available on retail store shelves at the lowest possible cost?" The ability to provide a very high level of customer service in filling store shelves by working with retail customers as infopartners is something that other companies cannot easily clone. When you excel at filling the distribution pipeline consistently, with the right amount of inventory at the right place at the right time, you can be sure of gaining a real competitive advantage, one that can be further developed and sustained over the long haul.

MEASURING THE RIGHT THINGS

As more companies take the plunge, it will become especially important for pipeline partners to agree on what should be tracked, measured, and reported, so that everyone knows how they're performing, and whether they're making progress, standing still, or moving backwards. Infopartners must therefore agree to performance measures that genuinely reflect the reality of a given distribution pipeline at any given point in time. Developing such measures will be a challenge for two reasons.

First, the campaign involves convincing people from different companies that common performance measures are necessary. Second, the companies have to reach a consensus on common performance measurements.

The first challenge, I believe, will be easier to meet—anyone who has participated in the development and implementation of major programs and/or systems will attest to the fact that to manage a project, one must be able to measure it. And with measurement comes control. It's not that difficult to explain this concept to others.

The second challenge, however, requires consensus building. In order to arrive at consensus about performance measures, the infopartners will have to focus on all the activities that impact product velocity and pipeline costs. The following lists map out the key measures:

Product Velocity Measures

- Inventory turn rates
- Customer service levels

182

- Sales forecasting accuracy
- Safety stock policies
- Lead times (procurement, manufacturing, and distribution)

Cost Measures

- Acquisition costs
- Manufacturing costs
- Distribution costs
- Sales costs
- Cost of capital

These measures, in my opinion, are the most critical in terms of velocity and costs. Of course, there are others, and as you think through your company's specific issues and concerns, you can begin to add to the list. Mine should be viewed as a basic starting point. The measures are what I believe are a minimum. With this in mind, it is worth briefly reviewing these product velocity and cost measures:

Inventory turn rates. Ideally, the measurement process should begin before the new system is in place, and continue well beyond system implementation. In this way, a valid assessment can be made by comparing "before" and "after" performance, and improvements can be seen. Calculations should be done using inventory valued at cost.

Customer service levels. Three service level measures should be taken: (a) product ordered vs. product shipped; (b) total order received vs. total order shipped; and (c) customer-requested delivery date vs. actual delivery date. For retail store operations, measurement (c) may be difficult to apply, but an honest attempt should be made to do it at the earliest opportunity. Remember, retail stores are customers and should be thought of as such.

Sales forecasting accuracy. There's only one sure thing you can say about a forecast—it will be wrong! The idea is to track forecast accuracy and set targets for reducing the error rate. For instance, let's say forecast accuracy, as measured monthly, was on average plus or minus 20 percent over the past four months. You'd want to set an objective to improve the accuracy of the forecast, and at the end of the year see how well you've done by comparing your objective to the actual forecast error rate. The only valid measure for forecast accuracy is selling units sold vs. selling units forecasted, by specific product package. Remember, factories, wholesaler/distributors, and retailers don't make and sell dollars, nor do they make and sell one product category at a time. So, for ECR purposes, national, category, regional, or dollar sales forecast accuracy does not count.

Safety stock policies. Safety stock must be measured if the company is to maintain a desired level of customer service. With a DRP-based system, such stock is easily measured, because it is completely visible for every product. Another important measure is crucial with safety stock: You should track how often you use it. Contrary to conventional inventory management practices, safety stock is there *to be used*. If, for example, you find that you have not used your safety stock for ten consecutive weeks, your stock levels may be too high.

Lead times. Three components of lead time *must* be measured, starting from the moment product leaves the production line: (a) order packing and loading; (b) transport time; and (c) receiving, unloading, and put-away time. Some companies also track a fourth measure: order preparation and release time. Other components might be uniquely important to your company; as a general rule, if something takes more than a day, measure it! In any case, each component must be measured independently, so you'll know where to focus more time and energy. Too often, people lump the components together and as a result they lose sight of the opportunities to improve.

Although these measures will give you an excellent reading in terms of how well you're doing vis-à-vis increasing product velocity, the next category of measurements—product costs—is just as critical as the velocity measures and should be tracked as accurately as possible. The cost measures category includes:

Acquisition costs. These are the total landed costs at your receiving dock. As in the case of distribution costs (see below), what is important is reaching a consensus. The objective is not to achieve elegance; rather, try to keep the measurement process as simple as possible.

Manufacturing costs. The key here is to focus on two specific components: overtime hours and line change-overs. The reason that these are important is simple. As ECR takes hold, if these costs are high today in your company, you should expect to see major improvements in both categories.

Distribution costs. At a minimum, the classic costs of warehousing and transportation should be measured. Depending on the company, distribution costs may already have been measured in great detail. What's important here is to reach agreement with your new partners as to which components are the most critical, then maintain a consistent pattern of measurement.

Sales costs. This is the cost of servicing your accounts. In addition to this classical measure, an attempt should be made to measure how much time is spent by your sales force selling product versus all their other activities. The reason is that as infopartnering reaches a critical mass of customers, you should begin to experience an increase in available selling time. As an infopartner, you will find a reduction in the time spent by your salespeople in activities associated with ordering and shipping product.

Cost of capital. This is the cost of tying up working capital in inventory. This measure should be done in the same way that you normally calculate the cost of working capital in your company. The key is to be consistent over time.

Taking all of these measurements in a timely and accurate way can be a challenge, especially if you don't have a good measurement systems in place already. Even so, it's essential that you have the capability to obtain accurate data on the basic product velocity and product cost measures, and that you and your pipeline partners agree about the methodology that will be used. This will enable you to improve performance in the context of your infopartnerships, and provide you with the hard facts you need to back up your claims. And if improvement is not forthcoming, by having a proper measurement system in place, you'll be in a position to take appropriate corrective action. Finally, it's important to note that activity-based costing is receiving wide acceptance as the premier method of cost measurement. As distribution pipelines are extremely sensitive to volume variations, I believe activity-based costing is ideally suited to track and monitor distribution costs.

TRANSFORMING LEADERS INTO COACHES

As I discussed so far, a drive for ECR success starts at the very top of the organization: *Unless top management believes in ECR and has a genuine desire for change, ERC will never become a reality.* Top executives must create a climate for change for ECR to work. That means much more than supporting ECR conceptually; top managers must get down to a detail level of the planning—which is something that senior executives often shun; they expect people in lower echelons to come up with solutions. With some efforts that can work. But not with ECR. Top executives need to come down from their urban towers and "get some dirt under their fingernails." That's the only way that they will effectively lead their companies on to ECR.

These top managers will need to become more like coaches—making sure that their players practice and receive the right training, picking the plays, bolstering enthusiasm, and so on. The ECR coach does the same, by creating a climate for moving the organization from where it is today to where it wants to be in the future.

In his book *The Phoenix Agenda: Power to Transform the Workplace* (Oliver Wight, 1993), management consultant John Whiteside refers to this new leadership process as "transformational coaching." According to Whiteside, transformational coaching is necessary when:

1. You're attempting a seemingly impossible task.
2. You're striving for ever-higher levels of accomplishment.
3. You have a history of broken promises and commitments to yourself and others.
4. You are overwhelmed by the demands of everyday business and personal life.

We badly need champions of the ECR vision to step out of the executive suites and become transformational coaches. That's how the ECR game will ultimately be won or lost.

It's time now to switch into action mode. We've studied our problems long enough, and don't need any more reports to tell us what's wrong. We know what needs fixing and how to fix it. The faster we confront our challenges head on, the faster we'll be able to realize the opportunities that await us in achieving the ECR pipeline.

Epilogue

Coming to a Mall Near You: Twenty-First-Century Cybershopping

Date: The last week of January 2006
Time: 11:30 A.M. EST
Place: A small town in the U.S.A.

Roy, our hero from the Introduction, sits at his breakfast table, watching the gently falling snow cover his lawn.

"Good thing we're only getting a dusting—the storm could have put the kibosh on our Super Bowl party this afternoon," Roy comments to his wife Martha, who's busily rummaging through the pantry.

"Uh-huh," Martha replies as she moves boxes and jars in search of appetizers and fixings for finger foods. "But we're not going to have any party unless we get some food. I can't believe we're out of so many things!"

Too bad for Roy and Martha—there's so much to do and so little time before they host the Super Bowl bash of the decade, in honor of the fortieth year of the venerable sporting event. Fortunately, in the twentieth-first century, shopping is as easy as . . . sitting down in front of the home planning center (referred to as the "television set" in the previous century). Roy and Martha do just that.

From the couch in the couple's family room, Roy uses the remote pointing device to activate the 72″ by 72″ high-resolution, flat color screen on the opposite wall. Roy places the planning center's keyboard on his lap and punches in the items they'll need for the party: beer, wine, soft drinks, pretzels, dips, and other snack foods. "Better add coffee and light cream to the list, too, dear," Martha suggests; "I think we're running low. In fact, we might as well get the week's shopping done now while we're at it. Make sure we get some extra chicken for Wednesday—we're having the Bakers over."

For the next five minutes Martha rattles off a list of staples, dairy products, main course ingredients, paper and laundry products, spices, and other items they'll need for the party and their meals next week. Roy carefully enters each one in the home planning center, using coded keys that speed data entry.

When he's finished, Roy hits a couple of keys, and is instantly transported to a "cyberstore" stocked with every item that the "real" store would carry. The images on the screen are as clear as a fine photograph. But they're far more than just a static picture; the items on the shelves are three-dimensional. Roy can "walk" the aisles by moving the pointing device, and can even use the pointer to manipulate boxes and jars if he wants to read labels. it's all so real that Roy's mind believes he's *actually in the store*.

Roy's shopping list appears on the right side of the screen, and has already been translated into a customized shopping route—all he has to do is follow the arrows on the floor, stopping as indicated in the appropriate sections to "pick up" (i.e., electronically mark) the products he wants to buy.

Roy maneuvers through the snack food aisle, then stops in front of the peanut section, as marked on his "shipping log," "Oh boy! Mr. Salty Snacks!" he says, smacking his lips. But before he can order his favorite party food, Martha snatches the pointing device from his hand.

"Wait just a minute, Buckaroo. Remember the old blood pressure. And let's check out the fat content while we're at it," she says, poking the pointer into Roy's bulging midriff. Martha then aims the pointer at a box of Mr. Salty peanuts, deftly rotating the container until she exposes the side panel listing the ingredients and nutritional values.

"Wow!" she whistles softly under her breath. "Almost a thousand milligrams of sodium and eight grams of fat per serving! The way you inhale this stuff that's three days' worth of salt and fat. Keep it up and you'll need a periscope to watch the next Super Bowl, 'cause you'll be viewing it from six feet under the ground. Here, let's get these Super Lite All-Natural Crunchies—they're salt and fat-free. The box says they're delicious, too."

"Yeah, if you're a termite or mountain goat," Roy groans. "What am I gonna tell the guys?"

Martha ignores her husband's grumblings and returns the pointing device to him, monitoring each stop he makes along the way. In less than ten minutes, despite two more nutritional firefights, the couple has finished their shopping. The system verifies that everything Roy has selected is available, tabulates the total order, and displays the amount due on the screen. It then asks Roy if he would like to pick up the order at the food-merchandising center, or whether he wants it delivered to his home. Roy checks "Deliver." Next, the system asks if he wants the charge directly deducted from his bank account, or if he'd rather pay the delivery person in cash. Roy opts for the direct deduction, turns off the planning center screen, then sits back and rehearses the excuse he'll give his buddies about the "delicious" snack foods he's about to serve up.

While Roy ponders his social fate, the store system is zipping along at incredible speed. Upon accepting Roy's order, the system generates an electronic pick list based on his selections. The list is divided into three sections. One contains staples—cans and boxes, bottles, and other goods that lend themselves to automatic picking. These bar-coded items are automatically placed on a conveyor belt and moved to an order consolidation area. The second section of the list concerns produce, snack foods, and other items that must be hand-picked. A store person batch-picks several orders at a time, including Roy's. Items are placed in tote boxes by order, and directed to the order consolidation area via conveyor belt. The third section of the pick list relates to meat and poultry. Roy's order for chicken is transmitted electronically to the meat-packaging center, where store people custom-pack the order, label and bar-code the (biodegradable) plastic-wrapped package, then send the package down a conveyor belt to the consolidation area. Within 15 minutes of completing his shopping "spree," everything Roy purchased is boxed at the retail store, ready for delivery.

At 2:30 P.M., just three hours after Roy and Martha "visited" the cyberstore, the order is placed on the next van scheduled for Roy's neighborhood. By 3:30 P.M. the order has arrived, and Roy and his wife unpack the boxes, put away the perishables, and place the (healthful) snack foods into serving bowls, well ahead of the big game, which starts at 6:00 P.M.

Roy might not have been pleased with his salt- and fat-free pretzels, but he was no doubt very happy about the convenience of shopping in cyberspace. The grocery store owners would have also been very happy about Roy and Martha's visit; electronic shopping would enable them to assemble extremely valuable micromarketing information about their customer base, and significantly improve their ability to forecast the amount of business that each of its stores will be doing. The same would be true for retailers in other trade categories, such as health and beauty, home appliances, home electronics, and so on.

With all the "point-of-consumption" information that electronic shopping could capture at store level, companies could develop daily profiles that helped them fine-tune their configuration for the best targeted investment in shelf inventory. Inventory itself would be a fraction of what it is today, because the closer you move to the point of consumption, the more you eliminate uncertainty. Electronic shopping would, in fact, virtually eliminate all uncertainty from tomorrow's distribution pipelines.

And tomorrow's distribution pipelines aren't that far away. What with the coming of the "information superhighway," electronically based point-of-consumption information will be driving a significant percentage of retail operations by the end of the decade. Retail stores as we know them today will be configured into multiple sections. One section—perhaps the main one—will be used for receiving and packing electronically placed orders generated by home planning centers or similar devices. The rest of the stores will remain pretty much as they are today; there will simply be smaller amounts of space allocated to "manual," "off-the-shelf" purchasing.

For those who find this a haunting image, one in which

people interact primarily with machines and "cyber checkout clerks," be assured that shopping as we know it will be around for a long time; the cyberstore concept will supplement, not render obsolete, conventional retail arrangements.

To be sure, "twentieth-first-century pipeline management" is a win-win proposition. customers can save a tremendous amount of time if they choose to shop electronically. Retailers will be able to service their customers better, and will have clearer information for managing their business. Everyone—customers and pipeline partners alike—will ultimately benefit from the costs being driven out of the pipeline.

Those companies that begin thinking today about the potential for using point-of-consumption data will be in the best position to take advantage of it when it does become widely available. They will also become models for info-partnering arrangements and the expert use of ECR. As a result, they'll gain a tremendous advantage over their competitors.

The technology for achieving exemplary pipeline management based on point-of-consumption data is rapidly falling into place. Why wait for the twenty-first century before thinking about how you'll use it?

Glossary

Actionable Information   Information that can be used for decision making.

Appointment System   System by which vendors can schedule a shipment at a retailer distribution center.

Available Inventory   Inventory in stock that has not been committed to a customer yet.

Bar Coding   A system of indentification using various bars of different width at varying distances from one another. The bar code can be read electronically by a specially equipped wand. The information is automatically stored in an electronic format.

Central DC   A major distribution center feeding smaller regional or satellite DC's.

Cold Turkey   To implement a system without testing it first through some kind of pilot or parallel implementation process. The system will be put on air all at once and this forces people to make it work.

Computer-Assisted Ordering (CAO)   A process by which the computer automatically reorders products for replenishment of stores or DCs. The CAO must be fed accurate POS and inventory on-hand data.

Conference Room Pilot   This is a tryout of the system where everything is real except that the system is not actually being used. It shows the users exactly what the output forms will look like, exactly how to interpret them, and how to work with them.

Continuous Replenishment Program (CRP) A process by which vendors manage the inventory of their products in the retailer's distribution center. Vendors receive stock status information from the retailer and calculate what needs to be shipped to maintain adequate inventory levels in the RDC. The "recommended buy" is submitted to the retailer for acceptance.

Cross Docking A process by which products from multi-vendors are received, handled, and shipped to multi-customers within a relatively short time span.

Cyberstore The electronic counterpart of a retail store, it will eventually be the heart of the "home shopping" concept. All products can be visualized in three dimensions on a TV/Monitor screen.

DC See Distribution Center.

Dependant Demand Calculated demand at the various levels of the pipeline. It is based on the requirements of the previous level.

Deployment Frequencies The shipping schedule covering the deployment of products from the factory to the distribution centers and from the DCs to the stores.

Direct Store Delivery Vendors (DSDV) Vendors who bypass the retailer's distribution center and deliver directly to the retailer's stores.

Distorted Lumpy Demands When the various levels of the supply chain are not integrated, uncertainties at each level are much higher than would be the case if the levels were integrated. The resulting safety stocks add up creating a distorted demand on the supply chain. This demand is not a true reflection of the market needs but more a reflection of uncertainties at each level of the supply chain.

Distribution Center (DC) Warehouses where companies with finished goods inventory carry their inventory so it is close to their customers. Synonymous with "branch warehouse."

Distribution Channel   The supply chain from the manufacturer to the wholesaler and to the retailer.

Distribution Resource Planning (DRP)   A supply chain has many inventory stocking levels interconnected with each other and strongly dependent on sales at store level. DRP is used to properly time phase the demands on finished good inventory from one level to another and plan production at the manufacturing facility to include the disribution system. It includes planning cubage and weight for traffic requirements, converting the distribution requirements plan into dollars, using it for planning manpower requirements at warehouses, etc.

Diverting   A process by which a retailer will sell excess stocks of products purchased at a discount. The purchaser (diverter) will then sell the same product in an area of the country where the product is not on sale.

DRP/CAO System   Distribution Resource Planning/Computer-Assisted Ordering system.

Dry Grocery Segment   The food industry's segment dealing with dry groceries as opposed to meat and produce.

DSD Fleet   Fleet of trucks used by DSD Vendors to deliver their products to the retail stores.

DSD Suppliers   Direct Store Delivery Suppliers.

DSD Vendors   See Direct Store Delivery Vendors.

Electronic Data Interchange (EDI)   Electronic transmission of data using established sets of standards.

Essential Information Triad   The breakdown of information into its three major time components: past, present, and future or past, factual, and operational.

Everyday Low Prices (EDLP)   The best possible price from a vendor on a continuous basis. As opposed to deal pricing where discounted prices are offered periodically. Also refers to a "no discount" policy.

Executive Torchbearer   A top management executive who fully supports a product/project and who will actively help in the selling and/or implementing of the product/project.

Glossary

Forward Buy   Process by which a retailer agrees to buy a given quantity of product at a given price from a manufacturer.

Forward Commit   Process by which a retailer agrees to purchase, over several periods of time, a given quantity of product at a given price from a manufacturer.

Forward Looking Continuous Replenishment System   A CRP based on DRP as opposed to being based on retailer provided stock status reports only. DRP requirements can be calculated by the retailer or the manufacturer.

High/Low Operator   A retailer/wholesaler/manufacturer who accepts/provides deals based on discounted prices.

Home Planning Center   Futuristic. A hypothetical home monitor/TV connected to various services through the "information highway".

Horizontal Mindset   A cross functional mindset as opposed to suffering from functional vision.

Independent Demand   The only demand that needs to be forecasted. It occurs at the point-of-sale to the consumer.

Information Alliances   The fundamental building block of Infopartnering. Process by which the various companies in the supply chain agree to share information on the demand for, and movement of, products.

In-Store Inventory   Product inventory in the retail store including product on shelf and in the back room.

Intrinsic Factor   Internal elements to the company or operations.

Inventory Record Accuracy (IRA)   Accuracy of inventory records calculated in number of units out of 100 who fall within accepted tolerances during a stock count.

Inventory Stocking Location   Various locations along the supply chain where inventory is likely to be stocked. Distribution centers are likely locations of inventory stocking.

JIT/TQC   Just-in-Time/Total quality control.

Just-in-Time An approach to achieving excellence in a manufacturing or distribution company based on continuing elimination of waste and consistent improvement in productivity. Waste is then defined as those things that do not add value to the product.

Live Pilot The system is used for a limited number of products only until users are thoroughly familiar with the system. The other products are added gradually until all products are covered by the system.

Lumpy Demands In an ideal world, demand would only be the result of consumer purchases. Maufacturers would endeavour to make one unit at a time for a smooth flow of products from plant to stores. In a real world, there are many constraints such as buying and manufacturing lot sizes, packaging and shipping lot sizes, etc. that cause demand to be uneven. Lumpy demand is the result of these constraints on the flow of product from plant to stores.

Manufacturing DC (MDC) Manufacturing Distribution Center.

MIS Management Information System.

MRP II Manufacturing Resource Planning—Material Requirement Planning evolved into the closed loop MRP system which then evolved into manufacturing resource planning. Technically, MRP II includes the financial planning as well as planning in units; it also includes a simulation capability. From a management point-of-view, MRP II means that the tools are being used for planning the activities of all functions of a manufacturing company.

Natural Linkages When the supply chain is viewed as a seamless pipeline whose objective is to move product from the factory to the consumer, the manufacturers/wholesalers/retailers are linked together by their need to move the product from factory to consumer as quickly as possible while being cost efficient. The need to move product from one end of the pipeline to the other is the glue that binds them together.

Phony Demands   Any demand in the supply chain that is not explicitly tied to consumer sales. The end-of-quarter quote "push" by manufacturers is a perfect example of "demands" imposed on the supply chain by a sales department only interested in meeting or surpassing their sales objectives for the quarter.

Planning Horizon   The amount of time, as measured by today's date forward, that is planned by DRP. The Planning Horizon can be as short as a few weeks and as long as several years.

Planograms   Shelf product mix placement as recommended by a shelf space management software.

Point of Consumption   The place where people consume the products they have purchased. Grocery products are generally consumed in the home.

Point-of-Sale (POS)   The retail store where the consumer purchases the product.

POS Data   Sales data at retail store level obtained through the counter scanner.

Product Flow Teams   Inter-company multi-functional teams whose objective is to speed up the flow of products through their level of the pipeline.

Rain Checks   To reschedule.

Raw Data   Untreated data, from many sources but mostly from POS scanners.

Real Time   As it happens. The present time.

Reorder Point   A quantity that is established for reordering purposes. When the total stock on hand plus on order falls below the reorder point, a new supply is ordered. The reorder point is computed by extending the estimated demand over the replenishment lead time and adding a safety stock to account for forecast error.

Retail DC (RDC)   Retail Distribution Center.

Retail Distribution   The distribution of products from the retail distribution center to the retail stores.

Satellite DCS   Distribution centers supplied by a central distribution center or the factory.

Shelf Management System   Software package that optimizes product-mix, placement and volume of product on self based on financial returns.

SKU   Stock Keeping Unit.

Software Pilot   To try out a software in a controlled environment, out of the normal business loop. The objective is to make sure that the software is working properly, that data has been handled properly, and that the numbers come out the other end properly.

Stock Keeping Unit   The identification of a product by name and number.

Supplier Driven CRPs   Same as Continuous Replenishment Program.

Total Quality Control   A system built into all phases of a manufacturing organization, from design engineering to delivery, that attempts to ensure that no defective parts are produced. The basic elements include process control, easy-to-see quality, insistence on compliance, line stop, correcting one's own errors, 100 percent check, and project-by-project improvement.

UCS Standards   Pre-established formats for the transmission of data through electronic data interchange (EDI).

Velocity   The velocity of products through the supply chain. Basically the number of days it takes for a product to go from factory to consumer or from any one point of the pipeline to another.

Waste   Any manufacturing or distribution activity that does not add value to the product.

Index

About the Author

André Martin is president and CEO of LogiCNet a division of Information Resources Inc. His company is dedicated to helping retailers, wholesaler/distributors, and manufacturers integrate their distribution systems from retail point-of-sale terminals to the suppliers' manufacturing facilities. Martin consults and teaches throughout the world in the areas of DRP, Quick Response, and Efficient Consumer Response, and has assisted numerous clients in developing world-class distribution systems.

As director of manufacturing and materials management at Abbott Canada, André Martin pioneered the development of Distribution Resource Planning. André was the driving force behind the successful implementation of the first integrated DRP/MRP 11 (Manufacturing Resource Planning) system in industry.

André has more than twenty-five years of experience in distribution and manufacturing. He is the author of the book, *DRP–The Gateway To True Quick Response & Continuous Replenishment*, as well as the Oliver Wight DRP Video Library. He is a member of the Council of Logistics Management and APICS (The American Production &

Inventory Control Society). He has lectured and given seminars throughout North America and Latin America as well as France, Great Britain, Australia and New Zealand. He has worked internationally with companies such as Coca-Cola, Colgate-Palmolive, Philips, RJR/Nabisco, Michelin, Digital and Procter & Gamble, and many others.